HOW TO MAKE MONEY WITH YOUR MARTIAL ARTS GYM

EVEN IF YOU HAVEN'T WON ANYTHING YET

PAUL HALME

Let's Tell Your Story Publishing
London

COPYRIGHT

This book is dedicated to my litter sister Jane Halme Larson.

She died way too young, aged just 34, leaving two small children.

She is a constant reminder to me to live my life and not take things so seriously.

When this book got hard to write, I would think of her and all the dreams she had that she never got to experience.

She reminds me that every day I can breathe, see my kids and kiss my wife is a win.

CONTENTS

ACKNOWLEDGEMENTS

There is no way this book would have happened without so many people. First would be my amazing family: My wife, Lori, who is the complete opposite of me and pushes me to be a better version of myself daily. My Mom, Anne, who I owe everything to; she built the man I am today. My little sister, Jane, who taught me what living is really all about. I miss her every day. Finally my amazing kids, Chase and Paige – every decision I make in my life is about them having a better future.

After my family there are some amazing people in my life who pushed me to share my message. Travis Lutter, my best friend who supports me in all of my crazy ideas and pushes me. Dan Meredith, who told me I had to write this book and share my systems. All of my students at Peak Performance MMA, who push me to make the gym better and not just a place about money, but family. My students who have become instructors, it's like watching my kids grow up – you push me to get better.

Finally, this book would never have been completed or been so good without my publisher Colette Mason. She kept me on schedule and when I would get burned out she would push me to keep going. Also a big shout out to my editor Greg Fidgeon whose ran his eagle-eye over my final draft and made sure it was ready to share with my readers.

To all of these people, I am so grateful.

FOREWORD

Are you f*cking kidding me..?' That, was one of the first things I uttered to Paul on our initial coaching call.

Now, before I go on to explain why this book could perhaps be one of the most powerful in your collection – let me give you a brief background on myself.

My name is Dan and I'm fortunate enough to own a variety of offline and online businesses, be a two-time bestselling author and have one of the most popular groups for entrepreneurs in the world.

I am also very fortunate to mentor Paul.

Now, there is one very good reason you should a) read this book cover to cover – and make notes and b) implement everything Paul says.

Why?

Because unlike many in the MMA/fighting arts space, Paul does not have a UFC career under his belt. He hadn't won anything when he was building up his gym from scratch (although he did go on to win a Masters BJJ World Championship in 2014 – 11 years after opening his gym).

But he has built a multiple six-figure empire in the BJJ/MMA space that not only allows his athletes to achieve great success but Paul himself has a life. Seriously, an actual life.

Unlike many in MMA gym owners who rely on their name or accomplishments to try and get business, Paul has learned the hard way what works – and what doesn't.

The sad fact of the matter is so many martial arts gyms close every year. All those dreams... all that hope... all that money invested... all the time that can't be brought back. Gone.

Paul can show you step-by-step how not to be one of the gyms that takes someone's passion and ultimately ends in failure, but instead have a thriving community of athletes who not only love you and your work... but pay the bills and more too!

In closing, if you are passionate about your sport but maybe think you are not a big enough name to 'make it' - I'm going to call bullsh*t on that. And if you want the 'edge' over your competitors its simple:

Ditch any preconceived ideas or ego. Read this book. Implement. And thank Paul later

Good luck

Dan Meredith

P.S. Why did I say, 'Are you f*cking kidding me?' the first time I spoke to Paul? Simple. Because he wasn't sure if people wanted to know what he wanted to share. And that's why you are reading this book right now. I may not be as tough as Paul but I'm a brutal coach – and a little bit of tough love isn't bad, is it? Ha.

INTRODUCTION

ABOUT ME

My name is Paul Halme and I opened my gym in 2003 as a brown belt in Brazilian Jiu-Jitsu with zero students and tried everything to get my gym to work. Lots of trial and error with so many ups and downs – but it was the best decision of my life.

When I opened my gym I was a nobody who had done nothing in the martial arts world. I was competing and training hard but not winning anything. This was a big risk to take but it felt right. I really loved teaching more than competing.

I was holding myself back because in my head I was no one. Then years later I learned that nobody cares about that, it's all about what I could do for them.

I had so many excuses why my gym wasn't making money. I hadn't won anything, I couldn't afford to spend a bunch of money on marketing. So and so is part of a big affiliation.

The first two years were so hard. I wish I would have had someone to help guide me on the journey and point me in the right direction. I had no idea what I was doing. I would put out yard signs and hope people would call. I kept working my corporate job as a stockbroker to fund my little school. This made for some really long days with a wife and two small kids at home. Without this stream of income, my school would have gone under in less than 12 months.

After two solid years of working at the gym, I was getting lucky and my gym was growing. I am a numbers guy and set up a plan to leave my good paying job once I knew I could pay all my bills.

I knew my broker's license wouldn't expire for two years so I could always go back. It was a bit of a safety net. My wife and I talked about it and we decided it was time for me to run my school full time.

In my fourth year, I was making progress but needed help. I went to a fitness business marketing event hosted by Bedros Keuilian. It was an amazing eye-opener. He opened up spots in his mastermind and I jumped all over it. Bedros was my first business coach.

I will never forget calling my wife and telling her I just threw down $10,000 on my credit card for a coaching program that we couldn't afford yet but I promised her it would work. I was not looking forward to the conversation when I got home and hoped to still be married when I got back. I am happy to say that I got to keep all of my body parts... Bedros taught me about direct response marketing, systems and internet marketing. I took what he used in the fitness industry and tested it, adapted it, tweaked it and refined it until I created my own systems for my martial arts gym.

Now we were off to the races. My systems transformed my gym and the school was busting at the seams. So I did what any lunatic would do and I decided to open three more. I bit that off way too soon but it was a good learning experience.

My next business coach was Lloyd Irvin Jr. He taught me how to get my gym to a level I never imagined. The copywriting and internet marketing I learned was legendary and got me into information products and DVDs.

Then I studied under Ryan Deiss, Frank Kern, Dan Meredith and Mitch Miller. I never stopped learning and still belong to various masterminds to improve my systems. This is what I will pass on to you.

Now the gym was profitable enough to let me travel all over the world training and competing. I had unlimited vacation days... lol. As I improved my systems, my gym became more and more profitable.

This was a big turning point for me. My school was running on all cylinders and I could finally train as much as I wanted to and chase some competition dreams. This culminated in me winning a Master No Gi World Championship at black belt!

WHO THIS BOOK IS FOR

This book is designed for anyone who wants to run a profitable martial arts gym. I am not too focused on having a mega-million dollar outfit. I chased that for a few years and I got lots of headaches and health problems. I did not enjoy that quality of life.

This book is for people who have a gym or MMA success, but perhaps not both right now.

Even though you have a gym, do you feel like people won't train with you because of your lack of MMA credentials?

Maybe you are a regular MMA person with a gym who has won a few things but nothing big. This is the spot I found myself in for years. But with the right marketing, you can amplify your position in your community and build a really successful gym.

Perhaps you are successful in MMA and looking to run a school?

Then this book is for you. I will guide you through the steps and systems to run a successful gym. You are going to blow it up when you try out these ideas.

WHY I WROTE THIS BOOK

I wrote this book for two reasons. Firstly, to document my crazy journey for my friends and family. The second is to help as many people as I can to run profitable martial arts gyms.

There is nothing worse for me than seeing gym owners struggling and knowing that if they would just implement a few of my systems then their lives would be changed forever.

Most unsuccessful owners don't know how close to success they actually are. Just a few changes and implementing a few systems is all it takes.

I know lots of good instructors who are afraid to put themselves out there for various reasons. They could make a huge impact on their family's lives and everyone in their community.

Get out there and grow your gym.

If I can help a few people avoid the hardship I went through for three long years and move them into the role of successful gym owner, then this book was worth all of the hours I put into it.

WHAT THIS BOOK COVERS

Over the next 11 chapters we are going to go over what you need to focus on to grow your martial arts gym. Since there lots of disciplines in martial arts – Karate, Jiu-Jitsu, Muay Thai, Krav Maga and more – to keep it simple, I will refer to all these types of a facility as MMA gyms.

1. WHY DON'T MMA GYMS MAKE MONEY

Many MMA gym owners set up their facilities with high hopes for the future, only to end up facing mounting debts and disappointment.

dWe will get the heart of why your gym is struggling by using a detailed set of questions to pinpoint exactly where things are going wrong.

It's a tough love chapter but will be the foundation of getting your gym back on track.

2. DEFINE YOUR MARKET

All successful gyms have worked out how to make their facility appeal to a specific set of students in their local area.

The first step on attracting those people to join your gym is to know who they are, what they are like as people, and what they want to achieve.

You will learn the process that I used to profile my ideal customers and make sure my website and my advertisements make a compelling offer to them.

3. WRITE A CLEAR AND COMPELLING MESSAGE

Once you know who you want to attract, the next step is working out how to tell them clearly how you can help them so that prospective students are itching to join.

You will learn the structure you need to use, including killer headlines and tempting bullet points that quickly explain to people what's great about what you do.

This system will work on your website, your flyers, your advertising and your face-to-face consultations.

I'll also show you how to test your messages so you can refine them and make them better still over time.

4. HOW TO SHARE YOUR MESSAGE

This is where it gets fun! You put in the work defining your market and message, now it's time to deploy it to your prospects via your medium of choice.

Most people do this backwards and spend all their time working on the media, but end up sharing a weak and poorly targeted message – and then complain that advertising doesn't work!

I will teach you some paid and free methods you can use to tell people how great your facility is, so no matter what you budget is, you will be able to get more people through the door!

5. HOW TO CREATE A PROFITABLE WEBSITE

Your website is the focal point of your brand. This is where people will look to get more information on you and your gym.

Prospective students will always want to check you out on your website. After seeing an ad, driving by your gym or seeing a flyer, they will usually dig in to discover more of what you are about. Your site needs to look good, be useful and up to date.

Again, I will show you some free and paid methods to make sure you can act on this advice. Your website should be capturing leads to bring you in more business and not just looking nice.

I'll also share some tips on how to plan your website revamp to make sure you do it as quickly and easily as possible.

6. HOW TO HAVE A GREAT FACILITY

See how we are moving your prospect down the line to become a student? Let's look at what it takes to have a great facility that welcomes people.

Do not overlook this like many gym owners do. Yes, you want nice mats and equipment but that is just the start. The ambience matters too.

You know the saying that you only get one chance to make a first impression? Well, it's true. How welcoming is your gym? Does it smell good? Do you touch up the paint and replace broken items regularly? The best feeling is when people on their first visit tell you, "This is way nicer than I expected".

I have ended up running a bunch of gyms in the past, and without some solid systems that made things run smoothly I would have collapsed under the stress. I'm going to give you those systems so you can get your life back too.

7. HOW TO HAVE GREAT STAFF

This is critical as you grow your gym. You need good people to help you because in the long run, you can't do everything on your own.

Your staff members are the people who represent you and your gym's brand and core values. A lot of times they are the first person your prospects will meet.

I was a jack of all trades when I first opened my gym. I unlocked the doors in the morning and locked them at night – and everything in between those two jobs was done by me. That's OK when you're starting out, but eventually it becomes exhausting and stops you from progressing.

Most business owners would love to clone themselves and have the duplicates run the business. Of course that is a dream, but with some good instructions, processes and guidance, you can come pretty damn close to the dream.

8. HOW TO HAVE HIGH CONVERTING INITIAL CONSULTATIONS

Thanks to the research you've put in to defining your avatar and your message, you can now hook prospects with your attention-grabbing headlines, persuade them that you are the go-to gym for their requirements with your copy, and encourage them to contact you to book their consultation with your compelling call to action.

Now you get a chance to show them, in person, that your gym is the right fit for them and will deliver the results they are looking for.

The rate at which you can convert those visitors into paying members is one of the most important numbers that you have to track for the success of your gym.

You will learn my 10-step process that converts a visitor into a paying member – even if you suck at sales.

9. HOW TO MAKE MORE MONEY

Now you know how to turn your gym's finances around, we'll look at ways to make even more money and boost your profits.

The most obvious way to make your gym more profitable is by getting more customers through the doors, but there are other techniques you can use.

It is hard work bringing in new students only to see them leave the following month. You need ways to make them stay in the long term, so I'll share my killer techniques for doing that.

10. HOW TO TRACK KEY NUMBERS IN YOUR BUSINESS

Numbers can be boring and nobody really likes math (lol!), but do I love money math.

Make this a game and try to get a better score each month. Then watch your school and bank account grow.

When people hire me to help them with their gym, they usually don't know the key numbers that I need to help them. This is the reason why they are struggling and not growing as fast as they want. It's so simple, yet it's a task that so often gets neglected.

Many gym owners roll their eyes thinking about numbers, so I have built you a tracking spreadsheet that does all the calculations and monitoring for you – you just need to type stuff in! I can't make it any easier!

11. DO THIS STUFF!

Just reading this book is not going to fix the issues you face. To grow your business you have to implement everything I have taught you. Start and then progress one step at a time. Don't let it overwhelm you. Start off very small with one task and then add another and another.

Soon you will have a beast of a gym running smoothly. But you need to take action using the information I have shared with you.

HOW TO USE THIS BOOK

This book is based on the system I used to turn my business around and you need to follow these instructions to get the most out of it.

Go through this book in order. Each chapter builds on the previous one, so if you skip bits then the system won't work. By following each step consistently, you will have a solid plan to drive your gym to the next level.

Similarly, each exercise in this book is designed to help implement my proven process. Make sure to do them all so that you know your gym is running at optimal levels. Some of them will be one-offs, but others need to be revisited on a regular basis, such as tracking your numbers.

A lot of resources have been included, such as template advertisement flyers and "swipe files" I use to market my gym – make sure you use them.

Finally, the free strategies are not optional if you have money! Even if you have a bunch of cash to spend, implement the free strategies as well to build a solid foundation for your gym.

Using a mix of free and paid strategies minimizes your risk of relying on only one system to attract and retain customers.

LET'S GO

We are going to kick this off by talking about why a lot of MMA gym owners do not have business success and how to fix that!

WHY DON'T MMA GYMS MAKE MONEY

Are you sick of burning cash on a gym that is going nowhere?

You might be good at what you do and love the sport, but most of the time MMA gym owners do not have the business and marketing systems in place needed to be profitable.

Most of the time those running a gym are pretty good instructors, but that often does not equate to financial success.

Referrals can be huge, but you can't rely on them alone to build your business. Of course, you have to teach exciting classes but you need more than that to get to the next level

I see this all the time. People are pumped about the new gym, they put up a few posts on Facebook and then it just dies down. They don't have a system to grow their brand.

If you build it, they will *not* come – unless you let them know.

LET'S AUDIT YOUR GYM

When I meet with a gym owner, I ask them to show me their marketing strategy, their website and what's going on in their gym. Then I advise them on what needs attention to boost profits and get things running more smoothly.

For you, I've set up a simple questionnaire so you can give your business a thorough health check.

This audit will help you understand what's working well and what needs attention in your business. That way, you can focus on fixing the weaknesses in turn as soon as possible.

The audit assesses the most critical issues first – your customer base and how you attract them to your gym. This is the stuff that keeps your business alive. After that, you will look at longer term issues that affect how well your gym runs.

To help you complete the audit, I have created a downloadable form, or make a note in the book. It's your call. (Resource name: audit.)

Q1-Q4: YOUR MARKETING AND YOUR MESSAGE

A fundamental mistake made by gym owners is hoping their facility will appeal to anyone and everyone because they are simply desperate for paying members.

This is understandable when people are panicking for money, but it actually makes running a successful gym more difficult. You need to have a target market to appeal to.

1. Do you know what your typical customer is like?

   ☐ age
   ☐ gender
   ☐ profession
   ☐ marital status
   ☐ where they live

2. What do they want from your gym?

   ☐ fitness and conditioning
   ☐ weight loss
   ☐ competition
   ☐ socializing with friends
   ☐ self-defense and confidence

3. Thinking about your website and flyers, etc and the way you describe your gym and your programs, is your message tailored to appeal to the people you work with – *are you the go-to facility in the area* – or is it generic and bland?

   ☐ tailored and appealing
   ☐ generic and bland

4. Are you proudly spreading the word about your gym and how great it is for your target audience, or are you anxious and withdrawn?

   ☐ proud
   ☐ anxious and withdrawn

Q5-Q10: YOUR WEBSITE

One of the best ways to reach out to your target audience is with a clear and easy-to-use website that explains more about your gym and what it offers.

Let's see how your website is faring...

5. Did your website load within two seconds?

    ☐ yes – it was like lightning
    ☐ no – it was at a snail's pace

6. Does your website work equally well on a computer and a smartphone?

    ☐ yes
    ☐ no

7. Can customers find your contact details within five seconds?

    ☐ yes
    ☐ no

8. Is your email address clickable?

    ☐ yes
    ☐ no

9. Do you have a detailed contact form that encourages visitors to tell you more about what they are looking for or does it capture the basics only?

    ☐ in depth
    ☐ basic – name, email and telephone only

10. Do you have any photos on your website to help people understand more about your facility?

☐ yes – there are pictures of students, trophies and a clean facility

☐ yes – but they are cheesy ones to fill the blank spaces

☐ no – not got any / not added them

Q11-Q14: YOUR FACILITY

We've spent a lot of time online and thinking in our heads, now take us to your facility as it is today.

11. You need to make a good impression. Customers get annoyed when they find problems. Do you solve them before customers notice? For example

☐ torn mats

☐ torn posters

☐ broken toilet locks

☐ blown light bulbs

☐ trash on the floor

☐ overflowing bins

☐ equipment lying all around

12. When people look around your gym are there people smiling, talking to each other and enjoying themselves?

☐ yes – there is a great vibe

☐ no – it's dead

13. Do you have a clearly marked welcome area for visitors so they know where to stand?

☐ yes – there are signs up and seating
☐ no – they have to lurk nervously

14. Can people see what happens at your gym because you put up photos of happy students and trophies on display or is it a mystery what happens there?

☐ yes – there is a display area to showcase what we do
☐ no – we have nothing up

Q15-Q27: YOUR STAFF

When you first start out, you find yourself doing all the work all the time and getting pretty burnt out on it all. At some point, you will need to rely on others. How's that going for you?

15. Do you have specific roles and responsibilities for specific team members? For example, receptionists to greet people and instructors to do tours with visitors?

☐ yes – I have mapped-out roles and responsibilities
☐ no – it's chaos

16. Does everyone pull their weight with basic tasks like emptying bins and tidying up?

☐ yes – everyone pitches in
☐ no – some people slack off or I have to do it all

17. Do you do all the menial day-to-day tasks in your gym or are you able to delegate them so that you can focus on your business?

☐ yes – I have people to help me
☐ no – I end up doing everything

18. Do you know what traits to look for when hiring a member of staff?

☐ yes
☐ no

19. When you need extra instructors, do you look for people you know already or advertise and interview?

☐ yes – people I know already
☐ no – I advertise and interview

20. Do you have a documented system for training up new members of staff so they know how you want things done?

☐ yes
☐ no

21. Do your instructors follow your rules for how your classes should be run, from a teaching and a customer service angle?

☐ yes
☐ no

22. Do you have a team shirt or uniform so that the students know who's a member of staff and who is another student?

☐ yes
☐ no

23. Do your staff chat and interact with the students so that they feel welcome or are they aloof and not very talkative?

☐ yes, they are friendly
☐ no, they are distant

24. Do you have informal audits of your staff to make sure that they are doing things to your standards?

☐ yes
☐ no

25. Do you know how to give people feedback so that you don't alienate and demotivate them?

☐ yes
☐ no

26. Do you lead by example with your gym and follow your own rules?

☐ yes – I lead by example
☐ no – I cut corners and break rules

27. Do you have a system for recognizing a job well done with your staff?

☐ yes
☐ no

Q28-Q39: YOUR INITIAL CONSULTATION PROCESS

Many gym owners feel they are not sales and marketing experts. Having a solid system to turn an interested visitor into a long-term member is much easier with a polished initial consultation process. Let's see how yours runs.

28. Are your staff familiar with why people in your target audience would want to come to your gym and become a member?

☐ yes
☐ no

29. Do you know how many of your consultation visitors on average go on to become paying members?

☐ yes
☐ no

30. Are people greeted promptly and in a friendly way or do your nerves show?

☐ yes – friendly
☐ no – nervous

31. Do you put visitors at ease and quickly find out what they are looking for?

☐ yes
☐ no

32. Do you accurately repeat back what the customer has said so they can be confident you understand what they want?

☐ yes
☐ no

33. Do you have different styles of consultation tours to suit different visitor goals? For example, weight loss or competing.

☐ yes
☐ no

34. Do you ask open questions that encourage the visitor to tell you more or do you talk at them?

☐ yes – I listen to the visitor
☐ no – I talk at them

35. Can you tailor how you describe your programs face-to-face to make them sound an ideal fit for your visitor or you tell everyone the same information?

☐ yes – I can tailor it
☐ no – everyone is told the same information

36. Do feel relaxed asking people to become paying members once you have explained how great your gym is or do you seem anxious?

☐ yes – I am relaxed
☐ no – I am anxious

37. Do you have your price list and membership options professionally presented in a folder or on laminated cards?

☐ yes
☐ no

38. Do you have flexible payments, like monthly instalments and annual plans for the customer to choose from?

☐ yes
☐ no

39. Do you have systems in place to follow-up with people who don't sign up with you on the day of the consultation?

☐ yes
☐ no

Q40-Q46: YOUR SALES PROCESS

As well as signing up new people, there are two other ways you can make more money from your students. Let's see how you're doing with that.

40. Do you offer private lessons at a premium rate?

☐ yes
☐ no

41. Do you bring in guest instructors to give your existing members something fresh to attend and keep their interest?

☐ yes
☐ no

42. Do you get referrals and recommendations from other fitness-related businesses in your area?

☐ yes
☐ no

43. Do you have your own clothing line for your gym? Kit that sells rather than stuff that sits in a heap in the corner?

☐ yes
☐ no

44. Do you ask people why they want to cancel in case you can put it right before they leave?

☐ yes
☐ no

45. Do you offer refer a friend programs?

☐ yes
☐ no

46. Do you keep in contact with your members in between sessions using email or social media?

☐ yes
☐ no

Q47-Q59: YOUR NUMBERS

One reason gym owners struggle is they don't understand some key statistics that help them make better decisions.

When you are worried about sales, covering the bills and paying your staff, it's easy to take your eye off the ball.

Let's see how you're tracking the essentials...

47. Do you know your customers' lifetime value?

☐ yes
☐ no

48. Do you know your average monthly transaction value?

☐ yes
☐ no

49. Do you track your student numbers in a given month and year on year?

☐ yes
☐ no

50. Do you ever track weekly attendance and absence?

☐ yes
☐ no

51. Do you track your percentage profit?

☐ yes
☐ no

52. Do you check how many initial consultations are booked with you each month?

☐ yes
☐ no

53. Do you track your advertising spend?

☐ yes
☐ no

54. Do you know where your leads are coming from?

☐ yes
☐ no

55. Do you know much each lead costs you per platform?

☐ yes
☐ no

56. Is your customer ad spend significantly less than the revenue from new customers?

☐ yes
☐ no

57. Do you track your overheads? For example, rent, payroll, taxes, utilities, advertising and equipment.

☐ yes
☐ no

58. Do you track your shop sales?

☐ yes
☐ no

59. Do you score your facility for key features such as cleanliness, the amount of equipment that's in a good state of repair or the number of things that have problems?

☐ yes
☐ no

INTERPRETING YOUR AUDIT SCORE

You've completed the audit. How did it go? How do you feel?

It can be tough reflecting on why your business is struggling – but the good news is you have just taken the first step towards fixing the problems with your gym.

Once you know where the weaknesses are, you can use this book to work out how you will solve them.

It certainly wasn't easy when I started out, but I managed to turn my gym around and set up some new ones.

We will now work towards raising your audit scores. Each section of the book will tell you which audit questions are being addressed, so you can focus your efforts on the biggest and quickest wins.

Make sure you read, understand and apply the advice in Chapters 1 and 2 before moving on, as these sections underpin a lot of the remedies later on in the book.

Let's make a start, shall we?

DEFINE YOUR MARKET

Did you think I was going to start with some Facebook or Google ads? No. This is where everyone gets it wrong! But don't worry, it took me years to finally wrap my head this around. The Market, the Message and then the Media.

Unless you have a giant marketing budget, you need to pinpoint your target market. When you have this set-up, your ad spend goes down and your results go up.

You have to know who your market is because they are the people who buy what you're selling. Look around your gym at your current clients.

Market and message are critical. With a laser-focused market tied into your customers' needs and your brand message, you will be years ahead of your competition. These two together are so powerful that you can then use any media to attract new students. Chapter 2 is all about getting your message correct so that it ties in with your customers' expectations.

Your market will guide you in making the advertising and service decisions that will both save and make you a lot of money. It has a bearing on everything you do.

When in doubt, always refer back to check who your market is. If you're not sure, this chapter explains how to identify the people you want to attract into your business.

Avoid the temptation of trying to appeal to everyone. Many new owners are guilty of this and will take money from anyone – even those students they know are not a good fit and end up causing problems down the road, force you to chase payments and turn up late. The most successful gyms do not appeal to everyone; they have a specific market they want.

Your success depends on you choosing a smaller group of people to work with so they think, "This is the place for me." Your perfect customer should feel at home in your gym from the start. There will always be minor differences, and that's OK. But the new customers you bring in should be a good match with your preferred types.

It's very important to get this right first. When putting together their marketing plan, the top guys spend more time working out who they are going to help than anything else. It's definitely more important than messing around with the font for your logo or your color scheme.

If you've never done this before, it really is simple to fix once you do the research. Don't worry, I will walk you through how to do this quickly and accurately in this chapter. Good market research can take a long time, but if you put a solid afternoon into it then you will be way ahead of those who are chasing the latest marketing fad and wasting money.

HOW TO DEFINE YOUR MARKET

In a perfect world, who do you want in your gym? Seriously, take some time to think about that and let it sink in. Remember, it's a rookie mistake to try to cater to everyone. The more focused you are the better.

DEFINE WHO YOUR CUSTOMERS ARE

The easy way to do this is to run through some simple questions:

- how old is your perfect customer
- what kind of work do they do
- how much do their earn per year
- are they married
- do they have kids
- what are their favorite activities
- do they need to lose weight
- do their struggle to manage their stress level
- do they want to be a fighter

See how focused you can get with this.

Think about how car companies do this. Mercedes goes after people in a different market than Honda would with their minivans. Once you can define your market, you can speak to them in their language.

What sort of people do you want to work with?

Do you want

- a fighters' gym full of blood-hungry 20-year-olds

or maybe

- a gym of 30-something executives with lots of disposable income who want to train and have fun

I have set Task 1: Who are your ideal customers to help you research your perfect clients in full. For now, just focus on learning why this is so necessary and then complete the exercise.

This is important because when you are focused on your ideal customers rather than anyone who will give you money, you can avoid the soul suckers and cheapskates.

Even when you're struggling, it's easier to turn away the wrong sort of people when you know they don't fit your ideal target customer and your long-term plans.

You need set your marketing up to repel the people that are wrong for your business if you're going to stay sane in the long run!

Stay positive. If you're worried about your gym's income, the rest of this book will teach you how to make more money from the opportunities in your area and still work with people you enjoy being around.

DEFINE TYPES OF PEOPLE WHO WILL JOIN

Who do you want as members in your gym? Look at the programs you offer and what type of people you want in them. For example, the way successful gyms reach out to female clients versus fighters is very different. You need to be very clear about what you are offering and to whom.

Now you have narrowed down the people you want, let's describe them in detail to create a snapshot of what they are like, their circumstances and their motivations. Get as specific as you can. This level of detailed understanding will help you write the best ads and organic content to attract them.

Why do all this research? Well, you need to understand how your ideal customers want your gym to help them. It's not about *you*; it's all about them, their needs and what they want. What's in it for them is a fundamental question. They are looking for something specific and for gyms that will help them. You must be able to define this clearly – and in a fun and engaging way.

You will need to take a different approach depending on whether your program is geared towards adults or children.

PROGRAMS FOR ADULTS

Here are some key points to consider for your adult classes.

How old are they

What age groups of adults are you targeting? How old is your perfect student? Look around your gym and see if it's more young adults than middle age – that can be an important clue for you. Will you have mixed ages or break them up? Sometimes the younger students are fitter and more mobile, and the older ones less so.

What discipline they want to learn

Is there a specific discipline they want to learn or are they just interested in fitness? When you're starting out, it's best to pick one discipline and get it working well. Alternatively, start with a small range and quickly work out which is going to be the most profitable option for you. Do not try to run a wide variety of classes when you're struggling. You won't have the time, resources or ability to turn them all round and have them working smoothly.

Geographic location

How far do people drive to train at your gym? Don't waste money marketing your gym in areas that are too far for customers to travel from. Do you want to target affluent zip codes or poorer ones?

Gender

Are you targeting both women and men, or just one group? Do you have different programs that appeal to either or both? You are going to speak differently in a fitness kickboxing ad aimed at women than you would to men interested in Jiu-Jitsu.

Lifestyle and leisure time

Do they like fitness? Are they a UFC fan? Are they an executive and live in a big house? If not, what do they do?

Health and fitness

Are they into a health and fitness lifestyle? What places do they like to eat at? Do they already a regular gym membership?

Interests

What else does your perfect student like doing? What are their hobbies? What do they enjoy? Do they follow other combat sports?

PROGRAMS FOR KIDS

Although you want children attending your classes, it's the parents who will be paying the bills and running the taxi service.

Unlike adults, income and profession are not relevant for kids, so spend your time looking at their hobbies and interests, their gender and ages.

Once you know the ages of the kid students you want, all of your targeting will be based on the parents of that type of child. Remember, there will be kids that you love to teach and others that have you screaming running for the hills. It's OK to rule out children you don't want to work with too!

It might seem a bit convoluted, but a status as a parent is a great filter for online advertising. This means it's easier and cheaper for you to show your advertisements only to parents who fit your criteria. This is the holy grail of advertising – better targeting. You don't want to waste your budget showing your ads to adults who are childless!

TASK 1: WHO ARE YOUR IDEAL CUSTOMERS

I have put together an avatar worksheet to help you list out who your customers are and what programs they will be interested in. The first task in this chapter focuses on researching the people you can help and that you enjoy working with. (Resource name: avatar.)

Later in the chapter, in Task 2, you will be delving deeper into what makes your audience tick. This detailed information will help you create profitable programs now and in the future.

But before you get cracking, have a look at these two examples so you can see how much information you need to gather and what you need to assess Task 1.

EXAMPLE CUSTOMERS

Adults: BJJ program

33 years old, married, 2 kids, makes over $75K per year, lives within 5 miles of my gym and watches the UFC for fun.

Kids' MMA (parent)

Parent of an 8-year-old, lives within 5 miles of my gym, Makes over $50k per year.

DECIDE ON THE OFFERS YOU COULD MAKE THESE PEOPLE

Now, look at all of the programs you could offer. How would you characterize your ideal clients for those programs? Will you be able to reach those people in sufficient numbers in the geographic location you're targeting? Will they have the money to pay you? Which program looks the best choice for turning your gym around quickly?

HOW TO USE YOUR TASK 1 CUSTOMER RESEARCH

Now you have a basic understanding of who your customers need to be, you can do more in-depth research to build something called an avatar.

When I say "avatar" I am not talking about that sci-fi movie with the blue people. I am using it as a marketing term. (I saw you roll your eyes then when I mentioned the dreaded "marketing" word again! ☺ Bear with me, this is important).

An avatar is a detailed snapshot of your perfect student that you want to market your message to and have enroll at your gym.

So far you have worked out some basic facts about your audience. Now they need fleshing out with specific thoughts and feelings that flit through the mind of your customers.

It is this accurate understanding of what makes them tick that enables you to word your programs to look like the obvious choice for them.

By the way, I want you to use this "avatar" sheet as a living, breathing reference document. It is a crucial reference tool now and in the future. Don't just do this exercise once and leave your research material rotting on your hard disk! Keep refining it as you learn more about your audience and have more success. Keep it up to date with your long-term strategy for your business.

TIP: Whenever you are in doubt about how to create compelling offers and messages for your audience, go back and look at your avatar sheet to remind you of who your ideal customers are for the marketing campaign you're working on.

So, how do you create this detailed avatar? Read on...

DEFINE WHAT YOUR CUSTOMERS "REALLY" WANT

You might think when someone wants to learn martial arts that they get your contact details and phone you or drop by your facility.

And that right there, my friend, is why you're struggling.

You need to know exactly why they want to make a start. Do they want to:

- fight and compete
- lose weight
- be more confident
- make sure their kid doesn't get bullied
- be part of a new social group and meet new friends

You're not going to make your fortune putting out advertisements for six weeks of MMA lessons. You need to connect with customers on a deeper level.

When you know the real motivation behind why they are looking for an MMA gym, you can make your marketing messages (the wording) much more relatable to them. By speaking to their needs and wants you make a connection that you can't make with generic copy. They should feel like you are talking to them – that you "get" them on a really deep level.

When you have your market down, the offers you make should look like a no-brainer to them. They should feel like you understand them and have the perfect, tried-and-true solution that they are looking for.

The wording on your website and brochures – everywhere – should relate to who they are and what they want. Talk about their needs and what they are looking for, not what you might have won in your career or how many square feet your facility is.

Understanding your customers is the first step to getting a high return on investment for your advertising. You will spend less money to target your ideal customers because you haven't wasted cash sending out bland and boring messages that put them off you!

COMMON CUSTOMER NEEDS

To help you nail the details accurately, let's take a look at some of the most common needs that your students will have.

INDIVIDUAL NEEDS

GETTING IN SHAPE

This one is huge. People are bored with regular gyms and want to get in shape, but they don't care about competing and want to know if your gym can help them tone up and have fun while learning something new at the same time.

There will be lots of reasons why people want to get in shape. How about the desk-bound 40-year-old professional struggling to lose their middle-aged belly or the new mom looking to lose some baby weight? What might be the triggers for your tribe?

BOOSTING THEIR FITNESS

Why does being fit matter? What do they need to be fit for? Do they need to be more flexible? Are agility and speed important? Are they training hard in another sport as well? This could be your extreme-type person or someone who really wants to push themself and boost their conditioning.

GAINING CONFIDENCE

They are less likely to admit this, but most people are not confident that they can defend themselves or their family against a threat if they had to. Maybe it's a parent who wants to make sure their kid doesn't get pushed around. This is a powerful one.

MASTERING NEW SKILLS

Are they interested in learning new (motor) skills? Have they trained in other martial arts before? Are they stressed and crave the peace of mind and balance that can come from learning a martial art like Jiu-Jitsu?

MAKING NEW FRIENDS

It can be a lonely world out there. Are they looking for supportive people to be around and make friends with? Have they just moved to the area or lived locally for a while? Maybe they want to join in your social events outside of the gym like the summer barbeque to get to know more people.

GROUP BASED NEEDS

Not everyone will want to take part from an individual perspective. Some are more focused on the group and what it feels like to belong to a team. Here are some motivations for these people.

TAKING PART IN COMPETITIONS

Do they long for the days of competing? This can be hard to deal with as they get older and remember those fun days with the team. Or maybe it's the young guys who love to compete and challenge themselves.

TRAVELLING AND EVENTS

Do they want to travel to events as a group? Could you appeal to their adventurous side? Do they want to go to Thailand to train for two weeks with the friends they make at your gym? How about to a national seminar?

SPARRING

Do they want a hardcore gym where they can throw down? This may or may not be your gym.

TASK 2: DEFINING WHAT YOUR AUDIENCE WANT FROM YOU

Define what the audience you identified in Task 1 does and doesn't want from an MMA gym.

Again, here's an example.

BOB

Bob is 35 years old. He misses competing with a team. He works a boring ass job and his wife tends to nag him. He can feel his stress levels rise daily.

He is looking for a fun outlet that reminds him of what it's like to push himself. He wants to make friends with some new guys in his age group as the people at work are so bland and stuck in a rut.

He wants to lose the 25lbs he put on since leaving college.

He feels exhausted when he gets home at night and likes the idea of early morning sessions...

DEFINE YOUR AUDIENCE NEEDS

Go through and really delve into your audience's psyche. Reflect on how you felt when you first got started.

Think back to conversations you've had with your students in the past. Have a look through emails people have sent you and do a bit of detective work. Browse some popular threads on MMA forums and look at the conversations newbies, intermediate and advanced folks are having. What can you learn from that?

HOW TO USE THIS INFORMATION

Do you see how powerful this part is? I know it's going to be a few hours spent that might be a little less exciting than enjoying the latest Hollywood blockbuster with your best friend, but the best marketers spend the most time on this research because of the benefits it brings.

You need to combine the information from Tasks 1 and 2 – your demographic (factual) and your psychographic (thoughts and feelings details) research findings.

Like it or not, you are responsible for marketing your business – whether you do the legwork or brief someone else to do it for you. The good news is, once you nail this you are on your way to running a much more profitable facility, I promise!

This research is what you'll be using in the next chapter to craft a specific and compelling message that hooks your ideal clients and encourages them to become paying members of your gym – without being pushy, sleazy or salesy.

TIP: Walk around your gym with your description of your perfect students and see if your current ones match this. You may or may not be there yet, but you are way further ahead than someone who hasn't bothered and is desperately scratching around to make ends meet, taking money from anyone with a wallet.

CLOSE

You now appreciate the importance of not trying to appeal to everyone with your gym, tempting though it might be when the bills are mounting up.

The two tasks have given you a good practical and emotional understanding of the people who are going to join your gym and give you money – critical information to improve your bottom line.

You also know who you want to work with and who you don't – and why! Running a business can be stressful and the fewer idiots you have to deal with the better. It's much easier to make the changes you need to when you enjoy what you're doing once more.

Now it's time to create that compelling message that's going to make your gym the "go to" place for those ideal customers of yours.

HOW WRITE A CLEAR COMPELLING MESSAGE

Those gym owners who skip the marketing research often skip the message stage too. This will cost you so much money in the long run, so please do not repeat their mistake.

This stuff might not be as much fun as slapping on an RNC to win a tournament – but it will stop your business from sinking under the weight of its outgoings and get you a much better work-life balance too.

WHY DOES A GOOD MESSAGE TRANSFORM YOUR BUSINESS

A solid message will be able to hook your prospective clients and grab their attention among everything else that they need to focus on in their busy lives.

This is where you tie in all of the things your market is looking for. Remember, your message will also act like your friendly doorman who works 24/7 to repel the cheap, high-maintenance people who won't be a good fit for your gym or your mojo, and leaves you to focus on enjoying your work and profits.

You can use your message in many ways.

Firstly, you can weave it into your conversations. Always relate what you're telling them back to what they are looking for. Actively listen to the person, don't just "listen enough" to find a point at which to interrupt and give your opinion.

Listen to the verbal cues you're given, then use the words you will put together in Task 3 to make your gym sound like the absolute place to be. Talking on the phone is another time when potential students are looking for reassurance that your gym is going to give them what they want. If they are a good fit with your ideal customer criteria, look to get them to book a consultation at your facility.

Secondly, use your message on your website. You can't make your website all about *you, you, you*. Yes, that part should make up part of the story on your "about us" page so potential students can find out more about you and your values. But the lion's share of your website needs to focus on what the customer wants and how you can give it to them if you are to stand any chance of hooking them and reeling them in to become paying clients.

Thirdly, there are your flyers, which are a great way to get your message out there. Just like your website, your flyer needs to highlight the benefits the customer is looking for and how you can help them get those – in a lot fewer words! Boost your enquiry rate from your flyers by adding enticing photographs and imagery that will appeal to your target audience. There's no point having the under-five-year-olds session photo on a flyer aimed at your 6ft 5in cross trainers, is there?

TIP: I have given you templates of flyers that I use for my kids and adults classes. You may find it helpful to use this as a starting point. I have found them very effective for bringing in new business.

Finally, all of your advertising needs to have your message on it. It's a good idea to use different wording for each program and each demographic you are targeting. Your message can also vary slightly with seasons – *shape up for summer, avoid the holiday weight gain.*

TIP: Get one offer working like gangbusters before diversifying and launching your other programs. Getting the wording right takes time and effort. You can't fix 10 programs all at once no matter how worried you are about meeting next month's bills. Get your signature program working and then work on the rest you plan to offer.

USING TARGETED CUSTOMER LANGUAGE IS MORE SUCCESSFUL

Targeted customer language will always be more successful than generic words. Here is a table with two examples to show you just how different two people's thoughts about working with you can be.

20-year-old single guys who want to compete and prove themselves	35-year-old dads with money to spend and a belly to lose
They are all about competing and might want to be a fighter. They want to burn off pent-up frustration and have the chance to prove themselves real men. They crave the pressure of going head-to-head with an opponent to motivate them, plus a concrete deadline of an event to train for.	They are looking for a workout to lose some middle-age spread over a few months. They want to get out of the house or office for a change of scene and have some fun, active downtime. The idea of socializing with others in the group is appealing, but going to work with a black eye is not!
Appealing headline	**Appealing headline**
Have You Got What It Takes To Be A True Fighting Champion?	Lose Your Gut And Shape Up For Summer With Group MMA

These headlines work well for their intended audience. But imagine for a moment that you swapped them over. Even though both messages are talking about martial arts training, they just don't have the same appeal to the other group because these two types of men have very different "whys" for training.

A tightly-focused message that reflects how the target audience sees martial arts training will always boost the effectiveness of your advertising efforts. This means it costs you less to get more people into your gym – music to your ears if you are struggling. What's more, it also attracts more of the type of people you enjoy working with and repels the ones you don't, so it makes your job more rewarding... no more clients from hell.

Let's examine why your advertising costs to gain a new client are lowered. Brace yourself, there's some math ahead – and you thought talking about marketing was bad ;).

HOW TO CALCULATE THE RETURN ON INVESTMENT FOR ADVERTISING

Tailoring your message to a specific audience makes it more effective. To explain what that means for your bottom line, let's look at a poorly performing campaign versus a successful one.

Let's say you showed your "lose your belly" advertisement to the wrong audience – to the "be a champion" guys. What might happen? Typically, 2% of the people who see your advertisement might contact you (maybe you are the only gym in their area?). But a whopping 98% will ignore it because the message is irrelevant. They will look for another gym that does cater for people like them.

It costs the same to place an advertisement and show it to the right audience as it does the wrong one. If most people say "ugh, no way" you're wasting money. You need more saying "This sounds great, I'm in".

Ugh, no way!	This sounds great! I'm in!
☹☹☹☹☹☹☹☹☹☹ ☹☹☹☹☹☹☹☹☹☹ ☹☹☹☹☹☹☹☹☹☹ ☹☹☹☹☹☹☹☹☹☹ ☹☹☹☹☹☹☹☹☹☹ ☹☹☹☹☹☹☹☹☹☹ ☹☹☹☹☹☹☹☹☹☹ ☹☹☹☹☹☹☹☹☹☹ ☹☹☹☹☹☹☹☹☹☹ ☹☹☹☹☹☹☹☹☹☹ ☹☹☹☹☹☹☹☹☹☹	☺☺ A poor message means only two people out of 100 are interested in what you're offering – not really enough to fill a class, is it?

Table 1 Example of the power of a poor message

If you just run ads to people who don't know your brand (cold traffic) with no real targeting, at best you would be looking at a 2% conversion rate if you had a killer ad and offer. It's just not going to be relevant.

When I see an ad for feminine hygiene products, I am "out" no matter how good the offer is – it's not targeted to me.

When you put the right message in front of your market you should aim for a conversion rate of 25%. This will take some tweaking and split testing to get it working well for you and I will go over how you do that later that later.

For now, have a look at what might happen if you show your "lose your belly" advertisement to your "chunky monkey" 35-year-olds.

Ugh, no way!	This sounds great! I'm in!
☹☹☹☹☹ ☹☹☹☹☹ ☹☹☹☹☹ ☹☹☹☹☹ ☹☹☹☹☹ ☹☹☹☹☹ ☹☹☹☹☹ ☹☹☹☹☹ ☹☹☹☹☹ ☹☹☹☹☹ ☹☹☹☹☹ ☹☹☹☹☹ ☹☹☹☹☹ ☹☹☹☹☹ ☹☹☹☹☹ ☹☹☹☹☹ ☹☹☹☹☹ ☹☹☹☹☹ ☹☹☹☹☹ ☹☹☹☹☺	☺☺☺☺☺☺☺☺☺☺ ☺☺☺☺☺☺☺☺☺☺ ☺☺☺☺☺ A good message means 25 people out of 100 are interested in what you're offering – now you're talking!

Table 2 Example of the power of a good message

This example shows you why the market and the message are so huge. Without dialling those in, you won't see conversions like this and you'll end up wasting money – not a good place to be if your gym is struggling to stay afloat. Not putting in the work to refine your message adds another hole below the waterline for your business, rather than being the lifeline it can be when you get it right.

Take your time to get your message right – it's a marathon not a sprint in many respects. I recommend you allow more time to refine your message than you did for the demographics work. (If you are in dire straits financially, I have shared some wording in my "swipe file" that will boost the effectiveness of your advertisements, so you can rapidly make progress and still spend time making sure you're showing the right messages to the right people for you).

It's crucial to remember each of those extra 23 people that contact you could be a new potential subscriber to your business. When you know how much extra revenue your advertising efforts bring in, you feel a lot less jittery about throwing money at growing your business.

Let's say your advertisement for your signature program cost $500. If you only get two one-month memberships at $150 each then you just lost $200 on the front end.

But if you get 25 memberships for $150, you made $3,250!

What's more, you can now use some of that extra cash to fund more advertisements for your other programs for other audiences.

It really is a money-making machine when you get this right – that's why I want you to put the legwork in on this.

Now, do your numbers.

2	x	your monthly membership	= __
25	x	your monthly memberships	= __

Seriously, how much would an extra 23 members a month help your gym and your financials? How much would you be prepared to spend to bring in those new members? I am guessing the figure is more than you might have been before you started reading this chapter.

Now you might be thinking, *"Hold on! That's 23 enquiries Paul, not 23 sales. I suck at sales. That's why my gym is f***ing struggling! I'm not wasting money on advertisements – I simply cannot afford to."*

Fear not, you will learn a rock solid way to close around 75% of those potential clients using my proven "initial consultation" method in Chapter 8.

When you create a steady flow of leads to feed into a good sales system, you will finally have a gym that is growing to fit your dreams.

HOW TO CREATE A COMPELLING OFFER FOR YOUR AUDIENCE?

You were set two tasks in Chapter 2 that helped you to define who your audience is and what their "whys" are. I explained these bits of information are the cornerstones of your success. They help you create a message that will appeal to your potential clients.

Now you need to reflect on that information and start to turn those ideas into your message.

You will be shown a step-by-step method on how to write your message. But before that, let me give you a few tips first so you avoid a couple of pitfalls lots of people seem to fall into.

This is golden rule: *"You are not your audience."*

You might think "so what", but underestimate this rule at your peril. First and foremost, you are a gym owner and not a gym goer. And you're not a newbie when it comes to martial arts – you have a lot more experience than a newbie. You also might have started with a very different "why" to your audience. You might be a different age or gender to you ideal customer(s). Maybe you grew up in a better (or worse) neighborhood. You probably have a different taste in music or movies, or have different role models, values, beliefs and standards. They might be parents and you're not. You own your own business and they could have a day job, or work the night shift.

The bottom line is, you are guaranteed to be very different to your audience and that is why you have to refer back to that avatar sheet you created. By reading your avatar information, it makes it much easier to take on your audience's perspective, and write what you anticipate they want to hear.

The other thing to mention when it comes to your message is to never bore them to death with your achievements. If they want to know what a hot shot you are, they will google you. The average person just cares about what's in it for them. Adding all the stuff about you to your message weakens it rather than strengthens it.

HOW MANY MESSAGES DO YOU NEED

When you are crafting your messages you want to make sure you have a different one for each program you offer, starting with your signature program. Each message needs to appeal to a specific avatar for a distinct program; otherwise you're heading towards the dreaded 2% success rate that comes with a mismatched message.

What's more, even if you're only promoting one program to start with, don't limit yourself to the first message you come up with for that offer – the chance of hitting the bullseye with your first shot is slim.

You need to keep refining your message to make sure you are promoting the most effective wording to your audience. This process is called split testing.

The amount of effort it takes to get your message right can quickly escalate, especially when you're new to it and split testing alternatives. This is why you need to nail the message for your signature program first before you work on the others.

In a few pages, you will be set a task to try out a few options to see which message resonates best with your prospective students. When an offer bombs you *must* tweak the message.

TIP: If you already have some students who fit your ideal customer profile, ask them to give you feedback on your message ideas and whether they would have contacted you or signed up based on what you have written.

HOW TO CONSTRUCT YOUR MESSAGE

All powerful advertising messages follow a simple four-step formula that I want you to use. Don't try to be overly clever or creative and use your own weird and wacky formula. Just like swapping the eggs for chicken in a cake recipe won't give you a great result, swapping bits out of the marketing message recipe is equally doomed.

You want to create a tasty offer your audience can't resist.

Let's have a look at the four-step formula you need to use for your message.

headline + body text + call to action + imagery = a powerful message

STEP 1: HEADLINE

You have to hook them with the headline! Think about when you're scrolling through Facebook and something catches your attention. It's usually the headline and or the image, right? This is what gets you to stop scrolling and think about finding out more. The goal of the headline is to get you to read on.

Examples:

> **WE ARE LOOKING FOR 10 WOMEN IN DALLAS TO JOIN OUR QUICK BURN KICKBOXING PROGRAM.**

> **DO NOT LET YOUR CHILD BECOME A VICTIM OF BULLYING. FREE WORKSHOP IN DALLAS.**

STEP 2: MAIN BODY

Your job is to move the individual along the path towards becoming a customer. You have gained their attention with your headline offer; now increase their interest by telling them why your offer is a good fit for them.

When you did the avatar research, you found out what they were looking for – the goals they have (practical reasons for signing up) and their "why" (emotional reasons that make it a lot easier to keep their interest). Don't over complicate stuff – tell them what they want to hear.

Your body copy can talk about the pain they feel at the moment. In the case of our desk-bound 35-year-old dads, looking down and seeing a big fat belly rather than their toes will be a pain point. Show them how good life will be like when they get the result. But not just the idea of a trimmer waist, include the emotional drivers like not out of breath playing Frisbee with their kids in the park on weekends.

Your wording should be all about the benefits they will receive and what's in it for them. Relate the benefits to the training, don't just say the sessions last 60 minutes and run on Tuesdays as that won't have the same amount of power as those emotional hooks you get when you refer to their "why".

Tie in pleasure and excitement. They don't want the same old boring crap. They want new, fun experiences and they want results that matter to them.

STEP 3: CALL TO ACTION

Much like fishing, once you've hooked your prospective client with your headline and reeled them in towards you with your body copy, you need to land them.

Customers, like fish, never land themselves – they need help. With a fish, you sweep it up with a net or swing it into the boat. With a customer, you give them a call to action – a clear instruction telling them what to do next.

Remember, the whole point of the message formula is to get them to contact you or sign up online for your offer. Unfortunately, sitting at your desk hoping for customers to materialize out of thin air doesn't work, even with a great headline and body copy.

The presence or absence of a clear call to action will make or break your offer. Just like your headlines need split testing, so do the calls to action. I have seen massive boosts in effectiveness with simple changes to the wording.

You need to make it easy for your target audience to want to do business with you. There are two ways to go about this – the right way and the wrong way.

The wrong way is to sock them between the eyes with a cold, calculating "Buy my sh*t" message.

Buying your sh*t should never be the first offer. This is a huge mistake that I see all the time. You need to build a relationship first and you do this by giving them something of value first. When you take all the risk out of contacting you, people are much more willing to take the next step.

Instead of broadcasting "buy my sh*t" you need to make a "low barrier" offer. These make excellent calls to action.

Here are a few options. Which one are you going to implement?

IDEAS FOR LOW BARRIER CALLS TO ACTION

Use these to gain your prospect's trust rather than kicking them in the shins and expecting them to part with their hard-earned cash.

BOOK A FREE CONSULTATION

Have them book a free one-to-one consultation and never a free class. There are two benefits to this.

Firstly, consultations are better than a free class because giving away freebies tend to attract the cheapskates and time wasters.

If someone books up for a free class, there's a good chance they'll be a "no show" or just do the one session and then vanish into thin air because they have not got "skin in the game". They are not invested in succeeding like a paying customer would be. This sort of call to action reduces the effectiveness of your advertising efforts because no-shows and freebie seekers are not going to boost your profits. Don't do it! ☺

Secondly, a one-to-one consultation gives you an opportunity build up the value of your program(s) right off the bat. The free consultation takes a bit of the edge off. They are usually nervous to come in and this way you can work one-to-one with them and break down precisely what brought them into your gym.

You'll remember that face-to-face conversations are a great opportunity to tailor your message, in this case to one specific person and what they want to hear. This is very powerful.

On your website or flyers, you are speaking to a similar type of person. On a consultation, you can discover what that one person's why is, and customize your consultation exactly to what they want to hear. You can take a personal interest in them. Who doesn't love being listened to and that their experiences and opinions matter?

Your consultation session gives you a chance to build rapport when you find you have things in common. Perhaps you both have three kids or maybe you have won a competition that they are interested in taking part in? Connecting on this level will help you build a strong relationship very quickly.

Another benefit of the one-to-one consultation is that it is private. Group sessions can be off-putting if your prospective student is shy and self-conscious. If someone wants to join your gym because they lack confidence due to being bullied or they feel like a fat failure, then admitting that in a group setting is the last thing they want to do.

Once you have established the relationship during your consultation, answered their questions, dealt with their concerns and fired up their interest, then you can ask if they'd like to buy your sh*t and join your gym.

In Chapter 8, I'll walk you through this process step by step because it is such an effective call to action.

PAID CLASS: $20 TRIAL

I love this one. Give them the option to buy it online and it filters out budget price shoppers. It shows the prospect the value of your programs. I give the potential client gloves or a GI with the trial as a bonus.

Prospects that spend money on a trial are more likely to become a paying member since they have already given you cash.

OFFER A FREE GUIDE

Another option is to offer something for free that your prospect can download in return for their email address. This is called a "lead magnet" because it works well as a lead generation technique. When you capture someone's contact details, you can follow up with them by phone or email afterward.

When you offer a useful resource – a workout plan or a video series demonstrating self-defense techniques, for example – your audience has a chance to experience what it's like to learn from you without spending any cash. Again, it takes all the risk out of the situation for your prospect. Nothing is more powerful right now than video. Mix it up with short and long videos and vary the subject matter.

If they enjoy the free resource, there is a good chance they will sign up for one of your membership packages, especially if you do a one-to-one follow-up with them.

They can't help but wonder if your free stuff is so good, how brilliant will your paid training be?

STEP 4: APPEALING, RELEVANT IMAGERY

Your advertisement is not going to be just plain text. You will use clear and powerful graphic design techniques to strengthen your message. That will mean a particular font, a set of eye-catching colors and relevant photos and a clean, crisp, professional and easy-to-read layout to add more bang for your buck with your advertising,

Remember to make sure your imagery matches what your avatar expects to see – so that means no kids' class pictures on your adult kickboxing flyers.

TASK 3: CREATE YOUR MESSAGE

This is fun and will teach you a lot. On a notepad, start writing out possible ads using the four-step formula.

Try different headlines, body copy, calls to action and imagery. Then read them out loud and ask yourself if this would get your avatar to stop scrolling on Facebook or pause as they browse the local paper.

Make sure to check out my swipe file for examples that you can use. (Resource name: copy swipe.)

This does not need to be perfect. Many people don't even start this process because they are afraid they won't get it right. Nobody gets it right the first few times, that's why split testing is so important.

Copywriters, whose job it is to write other people's compelling messages, will write up to 50 headlines for one advertisement and see which one works best to hook in the customers.

You can't just write one version and expect it to work straight out of the gate. Get some alternatives, and see how they work together.

Once you have some message ideas following the four-step formula, show them to people and see what response you get. Ideally, the people you share your ideas with the need to be in your target market. If you can't do that, ask friends to read your avatar sheet and imagine how they might react to the message if they were that person.

Fresh eyes are very helpful, especially when you have come up with lots of variations. Even with the best will in the world, you can get a bit jaded with it all and miss something that is obviously wrong.

Once that's done, you can move onto the next task – testing your advertisements in the real world.

TASK 4: SPLIT-TEST YOUR ALTERNATIVE MESSAGES

This is not as bad as it sounds – believe me, it's way easier than algebra.

I want you to spend a little money to see what works with your real target audience.

Why?

Well, if you've ever grown some plants from seed you'll know you need to pull out the weak ones so the best seedlings thrive and to grow into strong plants.

Keeping the weak seedlings undermines the progress of the strong plants because they steal resources the strong plants need – water and nutrients. Similarly, bad advertisements steal your profits. They need removing from your marketing strategy as soon as possible so you don't waste your time and money.

You need start off small with this.

Just like the seedlings, you don't immediately know which seeds in the packet will germinate and go on to thrive and which ones will fail. You haven't got a crystal ball to predict the future.

It's the same with your advertisements. You need to give them some time to see what happens and then make a decision on which ones to focus your efforts and which ones to kill off.

For your advertisements, you wouldn't place an expensive untested message as a double-page spread in your local paper or set your Facebook Ads budget to be $1,000 in 24 hours just to see what happens.

A prudent gym owner will put a small quarter page ad in the paper or allocate a $10 Facebook budget to see what response a message gets. (Yes you read that right, you really can spend as little as $10 on testing a Facebook ad).

I recommend you begin with online advertising as it's quick to assess and change and you can start with a minimal budget.

You can view reports that tell you which online advertisements are the strongest almost in real time.

This means you can turn off the weak ones quickly and easily. Unlike the local newspaper, you don't have to wait until next week to try again if no one contacts you.

SPLIT TESTING FACEBOOK ADVERTISEMENTS

The best place to split test right now is in Facebook's Ads Manager. It's free, powerful and quick.

A simple way to start is to create an ad and then duplicate it. On the second ad make a change to the headline and leave everything else the same. Then let them run for a few days and turn off the losing ad.

Now duplicate the winning ad again keeping the same, effective headline for both advertisements. This time, you can change either the picture, the body or call to action. Let them run for a few days and again kill off the losing ad.

The key is to only change one element of each advertisements you want to test at a time, otherwise you don't know exactly what is strengthening or weakening your message.

Your goal is to keep tweaking your advertisements until there are no more improvements.

Ideally, you want a series of strongly performing ads so you can rotate them to keep hooking in your target audience. Why? Well, 75% of your audience won't respond because the time is not right for them or there's something subtle about the advertisement putting that particular person off.

But the next time they see your ad it might be the right time or just the right "why" message for them.

Now you have a winning selection of ads to your disposal – and you just out-marketed 93% of your competitors. Nice work!

If you want to speed up that process, here's how.

TESTING WITH THE FACEBOOK ADS MANAGER

To rapidly test your advertisements, what you need to do is to test more variants – changing just one thing in each ad and run them concurrently. But if you're new to all this, don't run before you can walk by trying to test 100 variants at once.

If you're desperately short on cash in your business, it's understandable to not want to spend say $100 on advertising to test the response to your messages. But remember, you could be bringing in 23 leads very quickly once it's working. That's 23 people who could quickly become paying members of your gym.

The sad fact is that the longer you take to get this right, the more money you hemorrhage on overheads and the more likely you are to go under. Try not to view your advertising as an expense, but rather an investment once it's working well. You can only get it to work by making a start and refining as you go.

ADVERTISEMENT TESTING ON STEROIDS

If you've got some advertising experience, you can do some serious testing in Ads Manager by duplicating lots of ads. You can swap out each of the four main elements in the formula with your alternatives to find strongest performers.

The goal is to stop those 98% of people ignoring your weak advertisements. You want to hook that extra 23% of potential students and get them booked in for a one-to-one consultation or paid trial session.

I recommend you make your variations in this order.

HEADLINE TESTING

This is the first thing you want to split test and you will usually see the biggest results from this one. (Remember to refer to the swipe file listed in the resources section. There are some strong performers in there for you to use).

IMAGE TESTING

Getting this right will give you the second best results. Make sure the picture appeals to your avatar. It needs to convince them to stop scrolling through Facebook. It's also quick and easy to test this one because you can just keep duplicating the ad and change the images. You'll remember from Task 3 that coming up with 50 headlines takes time. Swapping an image is much quicker.

CALL TO ACTION TESTING

This one is gold. This is where you tell them what to do next. You need to move them along the customer journey. Please do not just leave your call to action as submit.

BODY TEXT TESTING

Does the body copy appeal to them? Look at the bullet points. Which ones could get you a better response? Do you have a link to your next page to move them further down the customer journey in the body? Try putting in some dashes or asterisks to get their attention. You can change so much in this section.

DON'T CHANGE TOO MUCH AT ONCE

Start small and only swap one thing at a time. Once you get comfortable you can do more.

Test the headline until you get a winner, test the image until you get a winner, test the call to action until you get a winner and then test the body.

When you're new to assessing advertisement performance, looking at lots of similar variations can easily become confusing and leave you unable to see the wood for the trees.

Having two options and picking the winner over the loser is much less overwhelming.

SPLIT TESTING OFFLINE ADVERTISEMENTS

With your offline advertising, you'll need your customer to tell you how they saw the offer so you can track which one is working. You don't have the luxury of software to help you.

You've probably seen other company's advertisements saying enquirers need to mention things like the "January offer" to be eligible for the one-to-one consultation. This "code word" is how they track the inquiry came from that specific campaign and not another source.

You can also do things to automate your campaign tracking, like setting up different web pages with an enquiry form or custom telephone numbers to what is generating your lead. However, that's a lot more resource intensive and slower compared with the online advertising route.

Keep it simple. Focus on getting paying people through the door, and then try the more spicy stuff.

CLOSE

You should have a clear understanding of your audience, what sort of people they are, and how to appeal to them by doing your testing with online advertising. Next you can start to invest more resources into sharing your message elsewhere.

We need to get as many people seeing your message as possible.

HOW TO SHARE YOUR MESSAGE

This is where it gets fun! You have put in the work defining your market and message, and now it's time to deploy it to your prospects via the medium of your choice.

Most people do this backwards and spend all their time working on the media, but end up sharing a weak and poorly-targeted message – and then complain that advertising doesn't work!

WHERE TO PLACE YOUR ADVERTISEMENTS AND CONTENT

There are so many options, paid and free – Facebook, Instagram, Twitter, flyers, Google AdWords, your local paper, your blog, posters on notice boards and more...

Start by testing out one or two places and then keep adding media outlets as you grow your gym. Don't try to do them all at once and then burn out or run out of cash setting them up.

Some are better for some markets than others and that is fine. There will also be overlap, and that works to your advantage.

By using multiple media platforms your prospects will see you everywhere. This is called "top of mind awareness", which is great because when they do think of joining somewhere, they instantly think of you.

Some of the media platforms are free, while others cost money. You can use free, paid or both – it all works.

If you have an advertising budget, you can use online and offline techniques to reach your audience. Let's have a look at the options.

PAID OFFLINE TECHNIQUES

I know "offline" is old school, but you can put a new twist on it.

TIP: It goes without saying you don't want to be spending money on expensive offline marketing materials if you're not sure your message is appealing to your ideal customers. Do some online testing first because that is much quicker, easier and cheaper to test and fine tune.

FACILITY SIGNAGE

You need modern signage that looks good. This can be a sign above your facility and you can add window graphics.

Don't just put the name of your gym on your signage, include your core message, your signature offer and always have a call to action to get them to contact you or call in, just like an ad.

FLYERS

These are great to put up at local businesses that you support, or businesses that also help your ideal customer. For example, at sports massage therapist. Offer to put some of their flyers on display in your gym as they will be way more likely to help you if you help them rather than expect a favor.

Your flyers need to act like a silent salesman, winning over hearts and minds 24/7 and not just include a bunch of factual information you threw together. If you're creating flyers, have a look at my template in the resources section. (Resource name: Flyer)

BANNERS

A nice way to get your message out is putting big banners out on the weekends or at local events. Make sure to check with your city to see what they allow. Again, the places where you might want to put your flyers may consider taking your banner too – space permitting.

PAID ONLINE TECHNIQUES

This is my favorite type of marketing, because you can scale it and keep improving it.

SOCIAL MEDIA ADVERTISING

This is where the biggest return on investment is right now. It won't necessarily always be that way but you have to take advantage of where the attention is.

Social media platforms are always changing, so you want to be on as many as you can for your gym. Facebook, Instagram, YouTube, Twitter and Snapchat are just a few of the many platforms you can use.

Have you noticed how changeable it all is? Social media companies seem to come out with new features all the time. New platforms emerge from nowhere – many fizzle out but a few become household names. It's a never ending game.

You want to make sure you spend the most time on the dominant platform. Right now that is Facebook, but that could change and it probably will one day.

As well as platform popularity, you need to think about where your market hangs out online? You need to nail this in your market research so that you have a primary platform to target, but still hit the other ones to get the overlap. Right now the younger crowd is on Instagram and the slightly older on Facebook.

You want to make sure the images you use on social media advertisements and updates match your message to your market. This can be huge when you have women only classes or MMA classes, for example.

As well as the imagery, the text in your social media posts needs to be in their language. It's all about being congruent with your message. Make sure to use their language by reviewing your avatar sheet and checking it matches the right tone of voice, and also mentions the right "whys".

SEARCH ENGINES

Make sure your website is listed and ranking on all the major search engines like Google, Yahoo, etc. (We will get more into SEO in a bit). Make sure you have claimed your business listing on the search engines and that all of your information is correct and up to date.

ADVERTISEMENTS ON SEARCH ENGINES

As a minimum, you should start off with Google AdWords Express and then start up Facebook Ads. Go to where your target customer is searching for what you offer. Many people skip AdWords because it's not as sexy as Facebook, but this is a huge mistake.

If you're not sure what to do, get some help to make sure you get the most bang for your buck.

OPTIMIZATION

Make sure your website is search engine optimized so it shows up at the top of the results when someone does a local search for martial arts gyms and disciplines.

If you do not know how, make sure to hire someone to help you. You want to dominate organic results (the ones that appear on the left-hand side of the page in Google) because a good amount of people will skip the ads altogether and go to the top one or two search engine results. Make sure that is your gym.

There are some SEO tools and reports that can help you work out what the popular search terms are.

If you're using a WordPress site, make sure to get the free Yoast SEO plugin. This makes SEO super easy by evaluating how well you've optimized your pages. The plugin automates doing a series of detailed tests on your information and checking you've got the balance just right with your optimization.

You don't want to overdo adding things like keywords because search engines penalize website owners who go over the top with their tweaks. It will also point out where you're missing a trick with your site. If you're lacking optimization or have over-done it, Yoast will tell you exactly where you stand.

Majestic is a great site for seeing the links to your site and the links your competitor is getting. This is of vital importance if you're in a competitive city with lots of gyms. You can see their key links and get them for your gym.

BLOGGING

Despite what you have been told, or how you might feel, blogging is not dead. Google wants newly updated content on your site and a blog is the best way to do that fast. Make sure to check out the SEO blogging resource in the downloads I give you and use it. (Resource name: Blogging SEO guide.pdf.)

Struggling to get ideas for good blog posts?

www.answerthepublic.com is a great place to come up with content suggestions for your blog. Type in the martial art you offer and you will get a list of questions people are asking about that exact subject – and it tells you which are the most popular questions! This is important because you want to make sure you're writing blog posts about things that lots people are searching for.

You need to answer these burning questions to get the best results. Writing about dull and dusty topics no one cares about is a waste of time and it won't attract new customers.

DO THE FREE THINGS EVEN IF YOU HAVE A BIG BUDGET

Even if you have the money to spend on promoting your gym, you still need to do the following free things.

This will create a compound effect and you will get way better results than from just your paid ads alone.

Also if your paid ads accounts get suspended for some reason, you've still got other ways to keep sharing your message. It doesn't often happen, but it can.

The organic content approach is slower than the instant paid approach, but this is a marathon and not a sprint. Organic traffic provides a steady stream of free leads.

Focus on the long game while you are doing the quick paid campaigns too. This is where you will see massive growth in your gym. What's more, a blog jam-packed with good quality, helpful information is a brilliant way to build your authority and boost your credibility.

FREE MARKETING TECHNIQUES

We have all been there, lots of ideas and no money. This is where you get creative and put in the sweat equity.

I once used a credit card to get street signs I couldn't afford and put them out every weekend. Sunday nights were spent bringing them all back in so they wouldn't get stolen because I couldn't afford another set! Back then, I had way more time than money.

TIP: Not all the paid methods are super-expensive. You can start for 10 bucks. If you skipped that bit, go back and give it a read, especially SEO and blogging.

CONTENT MARKETING

WRITTEN CONTENT

Make sure to get written content out there. It's one of the first things to fall behind on when you feel under pressure. You need to be consistent with your content marketing, else people quickly forget about you.

Blog posts

Make it a goal to have at least one blog post done per week and shared to all your main social media platforms. Check you're doing that.

Newsletters

Make sure your email newsletter is sent out one time per week and that the unopens are emailed again at the end of the week.

VIDEO

YOUTUBE

This is the second biggest search engine, so make sure to be uploading videos to YouTube consistently. Always link back to your website in the description. Add your videos to a playlist as it helps get more views. You can also tag your videos and use keywords to help them get found more easily in a search.

FACEBOOK

Facebook video is the best way right now to get a ton of eyeballs on what you do at your gym. Make sure to upload the video direct to Facebook and not use a YouTube link. To get the most reach do Facebook Live videos.

Also, use good thumbnail images to mix up what your prospects are seeing from you.

INSTAGRAM

Just like Facebook, make sure to mix it up with images and videos. Instagram will get your message in front of a different market than Facebook. You want your message seen everywhere.

TWITTER

This platform is losing steam as I write, but it's still a good place to get your message out there. Local hashtags are a powerful tool to use. You can have your Instagram posts share over to Twitter to save time.

AUDIO CONTENT

PODCASTS

Here is a way to set yourself apart from your competition. Start a podcast and distribute it to your students and prospects. Here are a few ways to easily produce podcast content.

If you already have blog posts you can read them out loud and use the recording for your podcast. Your smartphone will have a free voice dictation app you can use.

AUDIO FROM VIDEO

A super easy way to get podcast content is to take the audio from the video content you should already be creating.

You can upload your video to www.soundcloud.com and it will strip the audio off for you, so you don't need any special skills or software.

INTERVIEWS

Interviews are my favorite and the best way to get good content for a podcast. You can interview students, trainers, experts, etc... Look to produce content that your market wants to listen to.

Use the free webinar tool zoom.us to record your voices or Pamela Voice Recorder for Skype.

ORGANIC SOCIAL MEDIA

You can kill it with organic social media done right. Make sure to be hitting your main platforms one to two times daily. Post and interact with people.

TIP: You can repurpose written items for the leading social media platforms if you find yourself falling behind, as well as sharing the content you are creating on your blog, or at your talks and presentations.

Put out lots of videos, which get a ton of reach for free. Use the market and message skills I have taught you to really connect with your prospects and students.

For me, it's not all about making a bunch of money. You get to have the best job in the world, helping people become better versions of themselves. Sharing your take on that process is very rewarding.

Update your business profile pages to explain how and why you are a good match for your audience and their needs. Make sure people can clearly see who you are and what you do. Make it easy to connect with you. On your profile headers and descriptions, you can add your phone number, email address and website of your gym listed.

You can visit mine:

Just Google Peak Performance MMA Keller, Texas and you will see it how a prospect sees it.

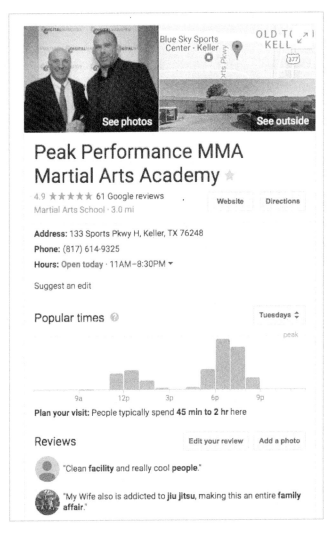

Use tools like www.answerthepublic.com to create content that meets their needs.

What does your avatar need to know? What do they want to be able to do? Write that out and start making content around that subject matter. Be the local expert they are searching for.

You don't always have to be creating fresh information; you can share other people's content. Look for interesting articles that your market would like and share them on your business profile. Give your opinion and ask them what they think about it.

Be real. Be you. Don't be afraid to get in front of the camera and talk directly to your audience. Your ideal customers want to connect with you. Don't post the same bland stuff everyone else is posting. Be yourself and throw in some pattern interrupts, crazy images, some personality and some opinion. This will help you to stand out from the crowd.

Your blog posts help you subtly share your values and beliefs with your audience. Are you quiet and thoughtful or loud and rebellious? Are you a calming, measured influence or a tough-love drill sergeant? The tone of voice in your blog posts should reflect that. This will help you attract the customers you're looking for and repel those ones you're not so keen on.

Whether it's your own original content or sharing someone else's, the whole point is to get people to engage with you, your gym and your brand.

Always engage with those who try to engage with you. Not doing so makes it look like you don't care. Reply to every comment and thank them for the share, etc... This will make your page so much more active and give you better reach.

Think of ways to encourage interaction. Ask questions to get people to comment. When they do, be friendly and approachable as they may be expecting the big mean MMA guy. When they find out you're a real person too they will warm to you and interact more.

GIVE TALKS AND NETWORK

Get out and crush the pavement. Press the flesh. Go and meet real people to spread your message and introduce yourself.

Give talks at schools, libraries, chambers of commerce, local business events. Set up a table for UFC events and support local businesses.

It is old school, but it works.

FIND A LITTLE BIT OF MONEY

Even if you're broke, you can find $1 a day to get more students from using the paid methods. If you can't do this then maybe running a gym isn't for you?

I can't even get dinner for two for under $30. I know you can suck it up and find $1 a day. Instead of buying a few beers and take out when you're feeling defeated, put that cash into your advertising.

Paid traffic brings leads in quickly, which is crucial when you have overheads cutting into the last of your savings. The longer you leave it, the worse your situation will become.

As well as helping to generate cash in the short run, putting money behind your ads speeds up the process of finding the good ones to capitalize on later. You can only refine your ads by running ads. You have to be bold, grit your teeth, rip the plaster off and start investing in your sales and marketing.

Remember, once you've struck gold with your ad wording, you will be able to get more leads into your business on demand – leads that you can convert into paying customers. The simplest thing to do is

---

look at organic posts on your Facebook page and amplify what is working. Yep, I'm talking about the good old boosted post.

Here is a ninja trick I got from Dennis Yu, who is a Facebook master. Look at your organic Facebook post insights and see what is doing the best and boost that piece of content for $1 per day. Let it run for seven days and then look for the newest piece of organic content that is getting engagement and boost that one. You can turn off the old one and you just repeat this every week.

This is so easy to do and will get you way ahead of your competitors. Just amplify what is already working. That way you don't waste money.

Now that you're comfortable with boosting text and image-based posts, I want you to find another dollar to spend every day boosting video views.

All you need is an idea to talk about and your smartphone and you're good to go. You don't need lighting and a studio, and a load of complicated stuff. Just be you, talk about a topic that matters to your ideal customer and get going.

Don't worry about it not looking too polished – the best way to improve is to keep doing this stuff.

Video is where it's at right now, especially on Facebook. Shoot a quick video on Facebook daily and post it. Then amplify the best video each week by boosting it, like the organic content.

For even more reach make it a Facebook Live video. Those are getting the most organic reach now and you will get great results from amplifying those.

CLOSE

This is a fun chapter. I enjoy implementing these techniques for my gym and I know when you follow suit you're going to see some great results.

Next up, we'll look at how to share your message on your website to generate even more profits.

HOW TO CREATE A PROFITABLE WEBSITE

Please do not skip over this area. Your website is the main part of your brand. It is where people will look to get more information about your gym and you.

If you scored low on Q5-Q10, this is where you'll learn how to improve.

After seeing your advertising or driving past your gym, prospective students will always want to check you out on your website. You need to ensure it looks good, is useful and that the information is up to date.

Many websites are like a sports car with no engine. They might look good but they are not going anywhere. All the information talks about the gym owner and what they have achieved – not about how they can help the prospective customer

If you have ever dealt with web designers and developers before, you know what I mean. They are good at coding and design but they miss the key marketing areas that a good converting site needs.

All the market and message information you've been refining in the tasks so far tends to be missing from a poorly performing MMA facility.

Even worse, there is no call to action or a way for customers to contact the gym easily.

As well as being easy to use and engaging, your website needs to be easy to search for by being optimized and indexed. Once there, you need to move them along from discovering you exist to building some rapport with you and to contacting you. This is called a sales funnel or customer journey. The trick is to have them take small steps, rather than rushing the process and scaring them off.

What happens if a guy walks up to a girl in a bar and asks her to marry him? He crashes and burns, right? The girl wants nothing to do with him. That's what a lot of websites do. They are asking the person to sign up to a program straight out of the gate! Just like any relationship, you have to woo your customers step by step with the helpful information you share on your website.

TIP: Repurpose the helpful information you put on your website and use it on social media. The more eyeballs that see your content the better.

WHAT A GOOD WEBSITE SHOULD DO

If the responses you gave to questions 5 to 10 have revealed your site is a disaster zone, you'll want to fix it. And since you've worked on your marketing and message, it's a relatively painless process.

CAPTURE ATTENTION QUICKLY AND EASILY

You need to capture your avatar's attention and guide them to take the next step – and that's it. You do this by including headlines that clearly explain the benefits of training with you and how it will meet their why. It's also a good idea to include images that relate to them too.

People seldom read all the text on a web page; they skim. That's why eye-catching, prominent and relevant headlines and images work so well. You can instantly grab your prospect's attention.

Your website should not be all about you and what you want to see on there. That's like being the crashing bore at the party, talking about yourself all night. If you've ever been around one of those "me, me, me" people, you can't wait to drain your glass and run away for a refill, right?

Also, don't waste your website's core real estate on your existing students. They have already taken that first step and you therefore have other ways to reach them than your website homepage. You can add "members" pages for your current students to find out information that appeals specifically to them.

CAPTURE LEADS

You need to have an easy way to capture leads, which are the contact details submitted by people interested in joining your gym. I prefer a site to have two to three calls to action so hopefully one appeals to your prospect. This needs to be an easy process for them.

Examples:

Click here and enter your information and you will get XYZ.

Click here and enter your information and we will contact you.

Click here and enter your information to get a free consultation.

PROMINENTLY DISPLAY YOUR CONTACT DETAILS

Ask a friend to go to your website and find your contact details – like your phone number, email address and physical address. Can they find the contact info in five seconds? If not, it's time to optimize. Can they find your phone number in three seconds? This should be one of the first things they see. Even in an online world a lot of people will choose to call rather than fill anything out on a website.

Think about how frustrating that is when you're on another company's website and they have buried the contact information somewhere obscure. People tend not to bother searching and will go to competitor that has the telephone number and email address in the top right-hand corner of their site.

Is your gym's address easy to find with information about travel and parking in there? Make sure this is clearly listed.

Put a Google map with their location so prospects can easily get directions to your gym. You want to make this as easy as possible for them to get the information they want.

You always want a company email address in your contact information. And make sure someone is checking the inbox and replying every day – just displaying it is not enough!

Avoid using a "Gmail" type email address. Instead, use one based on your domain name. It boosts your credibility in the eyes of your prospects. You can still set your contact email to forward to your Gmail so it's easy to check on your phone when you're on the go.

USE POWERFUL WORDING THAT INSTANTLY HOOKS PROSPECTS

Here is where you finally get the payoff from all of the market and message work that you did. Read through your site as it stands. Does it talk to your avatar? Can they relate?

Review what your site says. Does it explain what's in it for them? List the benefits that they will receive from training with you. Does that match your customer's "why" or is there a disconnect?

Just like an advertisement consists of a heading, some body text, a call to action and some relevant imagery – your home page should use the same approach.

Review the ads you created in Chapter 3, which will closely match the tone of the information you need on your homepage.

Follow the same basic structure for all your sales and landing pages. A sales page will lead to a sale if the visitor completes the action, for example signing up for a paid trial. A landing page gets them to take the next step in your customer journey. For example, fill in an inquiry form and request a call-back

SHARE YOUR CREDENTIALS

You can finally flaunt those credentials you have worked so hard for. Your message has got the prospect to research you instead of you cramming how brilliant you are down their throat.

In your About Us or instructor page, go into detail about who you are and what you have done. Time to brag a little bit because you earned it; this sport is not easy.

This will boost your authority and credibility, and help you earn people's trust.

TIP: If you're just getting going or are a lower rank with no credentials that's OK. You just need to massively boost the benefits the prospect will get from training with you. What are you exceptional at when it comes to your ideal customers why? For example, if you help people get in shape, share the before and after pictures of your students. That needs to be your focus as you build up your credentials.

DISPLAY HIGH-QUALITY PHOTOS

You need high-quality images on your website rather than low-res ones you took on an old camera. This is your brand 24 hours a day, 7 days a week. Spend the extra money to get good pictures. You can also buy high-quality stock images to use on your website that cost as little as $1 each.

Pictures and videos of your gym on your website need to look amazing. The human eye picks up on bad quality like torn mats, peeling up mat tape, dirty walls, worn out equipment etc. Make sure the facility looks in top condition in your images.

Double-check and make sure that pictures and videos of the outside of your gym look good too. Take pictures on a nice sunny day. Pictures of the exterior of your facility will appear on your Google Business Page. (More on this later).

Photos of your staff need to have them smiling and happy. This is no time for tough guy pictures. You don't want to run people off. They are scared enough about coming in as it is and looking for every reason not to. Look friendly and welcoming.

Student success stories and testimonials need accompanying photos. This is super important to developing social proof. No matter how good you say you are, it won't influence prospects as powerfully as social proof.

Your ideal customers want to see other people who have done what they want to do. It shows them that they can do it and you are the person to help them. Load your site with testimonials, including a photo or video of the person who gave it to you.

Ask your students to leave positive reviews on third-party websites like Google and Facebook too. This helps to get more eyeballs to see how good you are. Here are some questions and things to get them to say:

1. "Before working with [your name] my life was..........."
2. "How I felt before was............."
3. "Since working with [your name] my life now is..........."
4. "How I feel now is............."
5. "The ONE big difference for me now is............."
6. "What I'm really looking forward to is..............."
7. What tangible results have you achieved so far?
8. What would you say to someone looking to work with [your name] as a coach and why?

Get them to talk freely about the whole experience for just one or two minutes. Pop a Post-it note by the lens so they can refresh their minds as they talk, or print out the testimonials sheet I have provided in the resource section.

You can use photos to tell a story about your business and brand. People love to see success. Maybe there are pictures of you competing or holding a trophy you won. How about images of your old gym and the new one with all the upgrades or the picture of the group of students you took to Brazil? Those photos are compelling.

WORK WELL ON MOBILE PHONES

This is BIG. Your website has to be mobile responsive. It has to look good as good on a phone as on a desktop computer. It has to be easy to use and not fiddly and awkward.

People don't want to be zooming in to make the tiny text from your desktop-optimized site readable.

What's more, these days Google penalizes sites that are not mobile-friendly and shows them lower down in the search results – exactly what you don't want to happen.

If your site sucks on a cell phone, I've got some advice coming up later on in this chapter. It might sound hellish to fix if you're not a techie, but some off-the-shelf solutions work well.

WEBSITE OPTIONS

When you're looking over the options to get yourself a good website set-up, there are a range of things to consider depending on your budget and business needs.

First, let's review the key requirements you need for your new or updated website.

This is the number one place to show your message. Prospects will return to your site multiple times before they contact you.

Your website is not about you and your personal preferences – that is why your site is probably not working now right now!

The design of your site needs to be centered on what the customer wants to do and using language they can relate to.

The next most important thing is to make it super easy for them to be able to take the next step and contact you.

All three of the website options will work as long as your site is customer-focused and easy to use.

One last thing: Spending more does not necessarily equal better results. If you are tight on money or don't want to waste any more on your website, don't worry. You can get a good converting site even with a very modest budget.

OPTION 1: CHEAP AND EASY

WORDPRESS SITE WITH A GOOD THEME (FREE TO $100)

If you don't have much cash to spend, use a free website creation tool called WordPress. You can then select a template you like to get the right look and feel for your audience.

Check out the free themes first in case you spot one that hits the mark. If not, you can buy a quality template for $50-$100.

Have a look at competitor websites or any others that you like Sometimes it says "powered by" or "XYZ theme" in the footer. This can help you find something you like quickly and easily.

ThemeForest is a good place to look for themes. You can search by keyword or browse for the most popular. You can also pay a little extra for to get some help setting up and supporting your website with the theme developer.

Make sure you check out the demo site for the theme you're interested in to ensure it has the marketing features that you need – a home page, a contact us page, an enquiry form, a place to put your contact details in the header, different styles for your headline text, your body text, buttons for calls to action and so on.

It also has to be mobile responsive. Don't just do your research on a desktop – try the demo sites out with a smartphone too.

You don't want a website that is very text heavy. Remember, people skim read most of the time. You want to have a good mix of headline text, body text and images to clearly get your message across quickly.

Some templates rely heavily on fantastic imagery. Avoid these because they might look appealing at a first glance, but they are not very customer friendly for your purposes. Keep it clear, simple and to the point.

GOOGLE BUSINESS PAGES (FREE)

If you are dead broke, use your Google business page as a website until you have money to build your own. Make sure to update everything on that page.

As a bonus, when you link a good Google business page to a website you will get excellent search rankings.

You will also get your facility address and location marked on a local map, so it's easy for your customers to know where you are and get directions.

This is a potent technique – you must set one of these up, even if you have a website.

OPTION 2: DONE FOR YOU WEBSITES

SUBSCRIPTION MODEL ($100-$300 A MONTH)

The next step up is a done-for-you site. You supply all the information and another company builds and hosts the site.

These will run between $100 and $300 per month and usually have more features than a standard WordPress site.

They will often integrate marketing features such as page SEO and make sure all of your meta tags are right, etc.

These websites usually have excellent calls to action and easy-to-fill-out web forms for lead capture.

They will tie in your Google Analytics so that you can see how your website is performing and monitor traffic.

Another benefit of these sites is the technical support. They want you to keep paying so they usually stay on top of any issues.

The good companies will refresh the design as trends and technology change so your website always looks up to date.

OPTION 3: CUSTOM WEBSITE

FULLY CUSTOMISED SITE ($5,000-$10,000 - OUCH!)

This is high-level stuff where you are looking for a custom-built website rather than one off the shelf.

Be ready to put down about $5-10K for one of these. The good news is you don't have to make a monthly payment, so over time it gets closer in price to the mid-level option.

You should only consider these sites if you are already profitable and looking to get to the next level. They can be designed exactly to the specifications you want – although designers will argue about the direct response style and that's OK.

Good designers can tie in all of your sales and marketing systems.

Warning: You can spend a lot of money and get a site that does not convert, because nothing in this world is guaranteed. Make sure to research the company, look at existing client sites and see their results before you spend this kind of money.

TASK 5: SET UP YOUR GOOGLE BUSINESS PAGE

It's time to complete a vital task by claiming your Google business page and optimizing it.

It's very straightforward, just fill out everything they ask for and start getting reviews. This will put you way ahead of your competition as most people don't even bother to fill all of it out.

It is an excellent way to move your website up the search engine results.

If you've already got a page, give it a health check and make sure everything is up to date and reflects your marketing and message.

TASK 6: SKETCH OUT PAGE MOCKUPS

For fun – and to get your head around this – draw out some website mock-ups. Just grab a sheet of paper and map it out.

Box out areas where the text will go, and then do the same for the headlines and body copy.

Use some of your training from this book so far and write a killer headline in the box. Write out the body next. Talk about the benefits your prospects will receive if they join your gym. Put in a few bullet points and explain clearly what to do next.

What is your call to action? You can place this in the body text and also on your form.

How does your form look? Is it easy to fill out and what does the person get for filling it out? You need to capture emails. This will be one of the fields on your form.

Do you give them the option to book an appointment on your website? Where will your phone number go? Make sure on your mobile site that it's click to dial so it's easy for them to get in touch quickly.

I have put together a set of wireframes to help you. (Resource name: wireframes.)

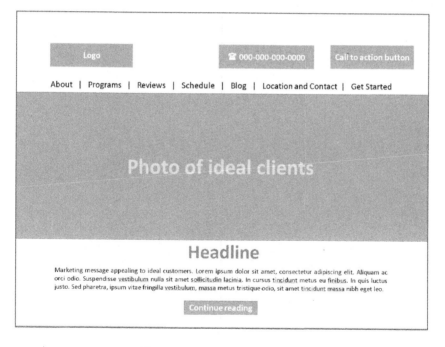

FIGURE 1 WEBSITE WIREFRAME

CLOSE

This can get a bit techie and in-depth, but you need to make sure you have a good converting website otherwise you're wasting time and money on something that is dead in the water.

What's more, an effective website works hand in hand with your paid advertising campaigns and your organic efforts to boost the return on investment for your marketing efforts.

Let's take a break from concepts and cyberspace and look at something more practical – how to set up a world-class facility in the real world.

HOW TO HAVE A GREAT FACILITY

You have now moved your prospect down the line to becoming a student. But you need to have a fantastic facility that welcomes people.

This is another area that many gym owners overlook. Yes, you want nice mats and equipment, but it goes way beyond that. The ambiance of the place matters too.

You know the saying that you only get one chance to make a first impression? It's true.

How welcoming is your gym? Does it smell good? Do you touch up the paint and replace broken items regularly? The best feeling is when people make their first visit and tell you, "This is way nicer than I expected."

Look at your gym it from the eyes, ears and nose of a new person coming in for the first time. Does it smell like sweaty gym socks or something a lot fresher?

Have you ever made an online booking for a hotel and ended up being bitterly disappointed with the place the instant you turn up? You're like, "This is so not how it looked on the website!"

You know the sort of thing – there's nobody to greet you so you just stand around looking at *stuff* to pass the time. Bad stuff. The wallpaper peeling off the wall, the crooked pictures that look about 200 years old, and it smells like a dog peed in the corner.

Eventually, you walk around looking for someone – anyone – who works there who can serve you. This is most definitely not the top dollar experience you thought you were paying for!

Now you're trying to figure out how to get your money back from the website because you don't want to stay there.

Does someone's first experience at your gym resemble this example? I hope not because prospective members will just turn on their heels and head for the hills.

TASK 7: CHECK OUT THE CUSTOMER EXPERIENCE WITH OTHER BUSINESSES

How well your gym is organized and how you greet and serve people is crucial. To get some ideas on how to get to the next level visit some high-quality venues and use some of their systems.

Apple store

This is one of the cleanest and most organized stores on Earth. Customers are always greeted right away and all of the products are displayed nicely.

They are all about service and making sure you are taken care of. No wonder they make so much money per square foot of retail space.

Five-star hotels

How different are you treated at a five-star hotel versus a two-star? You need to think of your gym this way. Nobody wants a two-star gym but that is what happens if you skip the little things. Start to treat your gym like a five-star hotel and keep looking at ways to improve it.

Mystery shopper

Go a bit ninja and try out other gyms in your area. They can be MMA gyms or regular ones. Book yourself in for a free tour. How are you greeted? How does their place look inside? This is how your prospective customer will be met too. Take notes and make sure you do a better job of it. If you're worried you'll get found out, send a friend.

GET ON TOP OF MAINTENANCE JOBS

You should be inspecting your place on a regular basis. Some things will need checking more frequently than others. Divide up what needs to be checked into a monthly and daily list.

These are called standard operating procedures (SOPs). They help you to do things the right way on a consistent basis.

Following SOPs is how big companies like McDonald's create the same set-up in all their outlets, so customers know exactly what they are getting wherever they are.

Your SOPs will help you to create the same, consistently high level of service and experience in your gym. As well as being great for improving the customer experience, they are great for you too. SOPs are the real secret to scaling your gym and giving you more freedom.

Once the instructions are written down, your staff can help follow them and it takes a lot of weight off your shoulders.

Here's the concept in more detail. After that, there is another exercise to review some of my SOPs to help you put yours together quickly and easily.

MONTHLY SOPS

There are the main areas you need to focus on to keep things running smoothly

- broken stuff
- worn out stuff
- missing stuff
- maintenance stuff

When it comes to monthly SOPs, a vital task is to inspect the gym and fix any problems. Look for light bulbs that need to be replaced or paint that needs to be touched up.

Even the smallest issues begin to undermine your customers' experience. Keep on top of that stuff to keep your members happy.

As well as looking for broken stuff, make a list of any worn out items that need to be replaced in the near future. At the end of the month, you can look at your budget and see which items you can replace or repair.

Stay on top of this so it's a manageable amount every month rather than putting it off and finding the costs quickly spiralling out of control.

Next is missing equipment. Are you missing things like a focus mitts or weights? Search the gym to try to find it and if you can't, put it on the replace list.

Lastly is maintenance and cleaning. If the doors, punching bags or chairs are squeaking, then it's time for some WD-40. Set up a pest control schedule and make sure this is getting done on time. When any staff member sees anything that is dirty, dusty or scuffed, they need to know to clean or fix it.

TIP: Your staff will always try and wriggle out of cleaning and leave it for someone else. Once a month, I do a walk through with them and address areas they are skipping.

TIP: Look for further improvements. As you do the monthly gym walk, list out things you can add or replace to make your gym even nicer. Look for ways to streamline what you do. Maybe you can stack things in a different area to make them easier to access and put away?

Customers notice and appreciate when you put in the work to make their training environment nicer.

DAILY SOPS

As well as the monthly tasks, you need to keep on top of things on a daily basis too.

The daily SOP is where the real magic is because they help you build and maintain a world-class facility.

Your gym is constantly in use and needs attention to detail to keep it spick and span. This is what creates a great ambiance for your members.

An obvious thing to focus on is your daily cleaning schedule. It's important to make it clear to staff that no one is exempt from cleaning. Folks need to leave their egos at the door.

What are the rules on taking out the trash? At my gym, it's when the trash can is half full. I never want to see one overflowing and it's everyone's responsibility to keep it that way.

A staff member should do a daily gym walk before the first class of the day and make sure everything is where it belongs and each area is straightened up. Someone needs to check the bathrooms too and make sure they look good and don't smell bad. That's a horrible first impression, especially for the females as the moms are the ones who usually bring the kids to class.

Pick up all the items left behind and put them in the lost and found. Nobody wants to look at dirty clothes on your floor and in your locker rooms.

TIP: Have SOPs for your website and social media as well. Although it might be in the virtual world, your website can soon get neglected and dusty – especially if you have event-based offers. Having your "January Special" offer on display in March is useless to anyone. Add in checking emails, your social media inbox and profiles to your daily SOPs.

TASK 8: CUSTOMISE MY DETAILED SOPS FOR YOUR FACILITY

Download my customizable SOP forms and use them in your gym. This will save you time from having to type them up. (Resource name: SOPS template)

They are broken down into office and cleaning. For monthly checks, I do a very thorough walkthrough of the daily SOPs to make sure nothing got overlooked.

ATMOSPHERE AND AMBIANCE

How quickly are people greeted at your gym? Is it by a friendly staff member or a grumpy ass fighter? Always be friendly and welcoming to customers on arrival.

(Remember my Google business page review? They said my place was clean and friendly. This stuff matters).

Greet new faces and ask about how you can help them. You have to remember how nervous people can be when they come into a gym for the first time. Make sure they are warmly received and that someone who understands your market and message is there to advise them.

But don't get the blinders on with your new customers and forget about your existing members. Learning their names and knowing their "why" makes a big difference.

Make sure to always greet them and talk about something that relates to them or their training. Show that you care and are interested in them.

Provide welcoming information on arrival. People are always nervous about turning up at a new gym.

A welcome sign or graphic on the door is an asset. Another is having signage outside that includes the core message your ideal customers are looking for. They will be much more relaxed when they know they are rocking up at the right venue, that you're open, and that this gym is going to be able to help them get the results they seek.

As well as sharing your message, put up photos on the wall of your lobby or entrance area of your existing members who look like happy, ideal customers.

TIP: Make sure to have a string of photos to fit each of your avatars. Newcomers want to see people like them getting the results they want. This is powerful social proof and helps get sales on autopilot.

Have a nice area to display your trophies and medals. People like to see that it's a successful gym.

Add a few text-based labels to your displays to make them more meaningful, using that all important customer-focused language. Always refer to how you help people reach their goals as your customers are looking for help.

When you take your prospective member on a walk of your facility, introduce them to staff members and happy students. A friendly environment will go a long way to making them feel comfortable.

DIVIDING ACTIVITIES INTO ROLES AND RESPONSIBILITIES

The SOPs will make things so much easier on you as you grow your gym. Everyone should know who is responsible for each task and how you want it done. You should keep them in your gym manual.

Think of a franchisee and how they have to do things the way head office wants them done. They are given a manual of golden rules they are expected to adhere to. Your detailed SOPs will keep your staff from trying to do it their way – or worse, shirking their responsibilities and not doing it at all.

Your SOPs are a simple way to clone yourself.

Make sure that you or a manager teaches each staff member what you want to be done and how you want it done. You should be able to disappear for a month and come home to a world-class gym just the way you left it – not a disaster zone.

SOPs will also help your staff act in the way you want them to if they have to handle situations or make a decision on your behalf – for example dealing with an irate customer who is demanding a refund.

By putting it in writing and having them sign off on it there is no question as to what they need to do each day. Everyone needs to understand what is required.

Think about what has to be done and the most efficient way to allocate those tasks if you have several staff members.

Some activities should be done by everyone – for example clearing up trash, promptly mopping up spills, or putting lost property somewhere safe. No one should be turning a blind eye and walking past this stuff.

Other tasks might be better suited to some of your staff but not all. Inputting customer details and printing off invoices, for example, would be best done by your back office staff. Front-of-house tasks like walkthroughs, initial consultations, completing liability releases and medical questionnaires should be done by you or your trainers.

I'll be covering this in more detail in the training section, in Chapter 7.

CLOSE

Now that your facility is world class, please make sure that you keep your staff on point following by following the SOPs. And if you're not sure how to have great staff, you can learn that next.

HOW TO HAVE GREAT STAFF

This is crucial as you grow your gym. You need good people to help you as you can't do everything on your own in the long run.

Your staff members are the people who represent you and your gym's brand and core values on a day-to-day basis. A lot of times they are the first person the prospect will meet.

When I opened my gym, I was a real jack-of-all-trades. After unlocking the doors in the morning, I did everything until I locked them again at night. Doing everything yourself is OK when you're starting out, but eventually it becomes exhausting and prevents you from growing your gym.

Without good staff, you'll never scale your business – or take a vacation. Having to cancel classes to go to a tournament or hope for a national holiday to have a day off sucks.

If you are still in the start-up phase and run ragged with endless jobs, don't worry – you can use my system to fix this.

HOW GREAT STAFF HELP YOU ACHIEVE YOUR GOALS

As a gym owner, you need to get rid of the menial day-to-day chores so you can focus on growing your business. It's hard to make sure all the essentials covered and still market and grow your gym. These unskilled jobs are the first tasks you need to pass on to your staff – things like opening and closing the gym, cleaning, basic repairs, putting up photos, handing out flyers and so on.

When you delegate the SOPs you will see how much more smoothly the gym can be run and your stress levels will drop. Spread them out so you are not doing everything – and neither is anyone else.

When you have more help, put someone in charge of customer service so you won't be the one having to deal with every email, phone call or minor issue. This will also speed up the replies to the students. Often when people get swamped, following up on service emails is one of the last things to get done.

By having a person dedicated to that task, you will see an increase in student satisfaction and retention. This also gives you more time to walk around the gym and interact with your students. The more smiling helpful staff members you have, the better the ambiance.

Remember, your staff are a direct representation of your brand. They relay your message and core values to your prospects and students. Have them wear team gear while teaching and always be courteous and helpful.

HOW TO HIRE THE RIGHT PEOPLE

Please don't make the mistake of hiring based on technical skill alone. Focus on character traits that you feel are important.

The worst staff members are those who are genius at something specific, but lack people skills and have a lazy attitude. Soft skills can't always be taught – people either have them or they don't. Choose cheerful, loyal people with potential and train them up in any specifics they need. They will be eager to learn.

TRAITS TO LOOK FOR WHEN HIRING

Look for people with a positive attitude. This is a big one. Negative people who complain all the time need not apply.

If you're considering someone you know already, make sure they are known as a friendly person around the gym. See how they interact with other students and prospects on a daily basis.

Another biggie to look for is honesty. Would you trust them to watch your kids or hold onto money for you? The last thing you need is a dishonest person working for you and your brand. If your team is going to gel together then mutual trust is paramount.

How do they come across when you meet them? Are they easy to get along with and fun to be around? What does your gut instinct tell you about them? No doubt students will feel that way too. You don't have time to train a loner or a bad ass who has no people skills.

LOOK TO WHO YOU KNOW ALREADY

Look around your gym – today's students are tomorrow's instructors. You can always hire outside of your gym but I seem to get the best instructors from my current students.

You can nurture a lower belt to eventually become an amazing instructor and staff member.

A great thing about your current students is that they know and appreciate how you run things. They have experience as a student and customer.

Equally, you should know them pretty well. You have seen them in class and how they treat people. You know they tidy up after themselves. You also have seen how they react to pressure and adversity.

Another big bonus is that current members are already part of the team and want to see your gym thrive. You can rely on them to be motivated and loyal.

HOW TO TRAIN PEOPLE UP

Once you have your candidates, it's down to you to train them to become a valuable part of your gym, either as an instructor or staff member.

Firstly, have everything written down. This should explain everything that needs doing and how you want it done – either in terms of running your facility or running your classes.

You have to be very detailed and clearly break down everything you want to be done, how, when and by whom. Don't leave any of it to interpretation.

Have two core manuals at your gym – an instructor manual that covers your classes, plus an operations manual that covers how your facility needs to be run.

Your instructor manual needs to detail not only the specifics of what you want taught but also the manner in which you want your classes run. This is vital to maintain the integrity of what you teach. Every instructor wants to teach what they like and that's not always what beginner students need.

Your operations manual will include the daily and monthly SOPs covered earlier, plus initial consultation forms, accident reports, etc...

Let's have a look at these manuals in more detail.

INSTRUCTOR TRAINING

Getting this right is one of the biggest ways to increase student retention rates. You should, at least, cover the following three areas:

- one curriculum per program
- client interaction
- general instructor conduct

CURRICULUM

It all starts with your curriculum. This should be what you want taught and how you want it taught. If you do not have one then your instructors will be left to teach whatever they want. You want the curriculum to be a direct extension of you.

You should have a curriculum for each discipline that you teach, as well as age-specific curriculums for children's classes. Ensure everyone knows where to find the manual and can access it easily. This enables all your instructors to look up what they're teaching if they need a quick refresher.

CLIENT INTERACTION

You need to train your instructors on the proper way to interact with students. They must to control the energy in class and make it a fun place for people to train.

Instructors need to be aware that part of their job is putting new people at ease. New students are usually very nervous and don't feel like they belong. Instructors need to make the newbies feel like they are a part of the team from the get-go.

Teach your instructors to spend a little extra time building rapport with your students. This goes a long way in making students feel like they belong and that your facility genuinely cares about them. A key component is learning their names and using them consistently. People love to hear their names.

STAFF CONDUCT

You want your staff to look good when they are teaching and representing your brand. A nice team shirt or uniform goes a long way and it helps the students know who to ask if they need assistance.

Make completing liability releases non-negotiable. This seems like a no-brainer, but some staff members may skip this and put your business in danger. A liability waiver will give you a lot more protection than not having one. Check with a lawyer in your city and get one created, and then use it for anyone who comes into your gym.

Go over your safety procedures when you do your monthly gym walkthroughs with your instructors. Do everything in your power to provide a safe training environment for everyone.

No matter how much effort you put into keeping folks safe, accidents will happen. It sucks but it's a part of martial arts training. Check with your liability insurance company and make sure to have staff members fill out the incident report that your insurance company recommends.

FACILITY TRAINING

That's covered instructor training, now let's turn to facility training. Things you'll want to include in this manual are:

- roles and responsibilities
- daily and monthly SOPs
- sales and marketing

ROLES AND RESPONSIBILITIES

Everyone needs to know what each staff member is responsible for. This helps with accountability and cuts down on excuses.

As your team grows, it makes sense to have different responsibilities for specific roles. With a large team you may have a front desk person, instructors, sales staff, and a manager and so on. It makes sense to have them specialize in particular tasks.

For example, a fundamental responsibility of the front desk person is to ensure that members and prospects log in. You need to track this data.

Some responsibilities will overlap across different roles, such as clearing up trash. And it's everyone's duty to make sure your rules are followed.

SALES AND MARKETING

You need to train every person on your staff on how to do sales. If you just have one sales person – i.e. you! – then you are extremely limited and won't be able to give the prospective members enough attention.

Running guided tours is an easy task to delegate even if you have a small staff. Teach your staff how to give effective tours of your gym if your main salesperson is busy and a prospect needs showing round. At the very least, everyone should be able to welcome the prospect and make them feel at home instead of just waiting in the lobby.

Get your staff to understand your avatar and the messages they need to hear so they can build rapport quickly and easily.

Everyone on your staff should be speaking and interacting with students all day long. You never know how close someone is to quitting. Your students deserve all of the attention they need.

Initial consultations are another critical area where everyone needs to be up to speed. You'll remember from the advertising advice that one of your best calls to action is getting people to book a consultation and visit your facility. There are no prizes for guessing that – sorry! – you're going to need someone to run those consultations.

As well as explaining how to run a session, you'll need to teach your staff how to get prospects to sign on the dotted line to become paying customers. You'll be surprised how good people who are initially scared of sales can get if you train them right, give them confidence and pay them commissions.

Have a look at Chapter 8 for a step-by-step guide on how to run the perfect initial consultation and get people to sign up with you. Trust me when I tell you I have refined this over the years. It works like gangbusters.

HOW TO GET PEOPLE TO FOLLOW YOUR PROCEDURES

You need to stay on top of your staff or they will start doing what they want. The challenge here is to not become a micro-manager.

There are lots of techniques you can use:

- random audits and constructive feedback

- leading by example
- collaboration
- rewards

HAVE RANDOM AUDITS AND PROVIDE CONSTRUCTIVE FEEDBACK

As long as you're doing consistent training you'll be able to keep an eye on things with random audits. Pick a role and responsibility and see how the task is being done. Always pick a different one to see the overall quality of your staff's work and not make people feel like they have been singled out.

When you spot something not going to plan, don't just jump down their throat. If you lay into them about everything they've got wrong, you're not going to solve the problem or motivate people to get it right. You need to give people constructive feedback. When you debrief them after the random audit, start by thanking them for the good things they are doing and then give constructive feedback on any areas that need improvement, before finishing with some more things they got right.

Delegate the task of checking if the manuals are being followed to the letter if you can. In the long run, you want a manager or senior staff member to keep track of the day to day. This prevents you from looking like a micro-manager.

LEAD BY EXAMPLE

It goes without saying that it's imperative to follow your own rules. Don't walk past empty water bottles or ignore new students. Your staff will do the things that you do.

If you need to reprimand someone for not following the rules, you lose all your authority if you fail to practice what you preach. There cannot be one set of rules for you and a different set for everyone else.

For example, if the phone rings and you're next to it, politely answer it. Let your staff see how important these things are to you and the success of your gym.

COLLABORATE

When you compile your first manual, the chances are you'll be doing it on your own. Over time, as your team grows, let your staff weigh in when you're putting together checklists and SOPs. Discuss areas that are working well and tasks that they would like changed. Empower your staff to improve the gym.

Get agreement rather than dictating the rules all the time. Nobody wants to deal with that. Allow staff to have a voice and impact on the quality of the gym. Make sure everyone is in agreement on the rules and tasks. This will make it so much easier to enforce when you have to.

What's more, collaboration lets you benefit from having more perspectives to put together better manuals.

Have you ever seen that TV show, Undercover Boss USA? The boss leaves the safety of the head office, puts on a disguise and goes back to the floor, rolling up their sleeves and working alongside the Regular Joes. Why? Because they learn a lot from the people actually doing the job, rather than second guessing how things should be done from on high.

As a gym owner, you can get disconnected from the nitty-gritty of day-to-day activities. By getting feedback from your staff you can see things from their perspective and if it helps the gym then you need to make the updates.

GIVE REWARDS

Recognize a job well done. When you see a staff member doing well, give them some public praise. Everyone loves to hear when they are doing a good job. You can even throw in random gift cards, etc. You don't want to be the boss who is always finding the bad things. Make a point of noticing the good things too.

CLOSE

You have rock star staff members who keep your gym clean, handle intro lessons, market and teach amazing classes – now you can show them how to deliver high-converting initial consultations to grow your gym.

HOW TO HAVE HIGH CONVERTING INITIAL CONSULTATIONS

Thanks to the research you've done into your avatar and your message, you can hook prospects with your head-turning headlines, persuade them that you are the go-to gym for their requirements with your body copy, and encourage them to contact you with your compelling call to action to book their consultation.

You now get a chance to show them, in person, that your gym is the right fit for them and that they will get them the results that they are looking for.

The rate at which you can convert those visitors into paying members is one of the most important numbers that you have to track for the success of your gym.

The better your conversion *rate*, the higher your profits.

It's one of the first numbers I ask for when I go into a gym. You can tell how successful they are based on this (and a few other key metrics that you will be shown later in Chapter 10).

You should aim for an initial consultation conversion rate of 70-80%. Most gyms I start working with are usually around 50% or lower.

In Chapter 3 you learned about how your website wording affects the number of people who will book a consultation. Now you will find out how to communicate with your visitors when they arrive for their session so you can convert more of those leads into paying customers and higher profits.

This has a dramatic effect on your profitability, as this example will show.

NUMBERS CAN BE EXCITING

Imagine you had a decent month and 20 appointments show up:

- at 50% conversion, you have 10 new students
- at 75% conversion you have 15 new students

It doesn't seem big until you delve into the numbers.

Five extra students per month with a monthly average of $150 is $750.

If the average student stays seven months, that's an additional $5,250 to the bottom line.

Do that every month and you just added $63,000 to your annual sales. Excited now, huh?

THE KILLER CONSULTATION FORMULA

Here are all the elements you need to have in place to boost your consultation conversion rate. There is a template consultation form in the resources section to help you create a system for your gym.

STEP 1: HAVE A STRONG GREETING

Prospects need to be met and greeted quickly and in a friendly manner. They can easily turn on their heels and walk out if no one is paying attention to them.

Visitors need to be welcomed by someone with a smile and a positive attitude. Have you ever been into a store to be faced by a grumpy staff member? It puts you off going in there instantly. Don't let this happen at your gym.

Be real and not over the top. It's important to appear relaxed, confident and above all genuine if you're going to gain their trust.

Most of your first-time visitors are nervous to even be coming into your gym, so your first priority is to put them at ease to stop them backing out before you've even started the session.

Staff at the front desk need to look presentable and not like a homeless person. The person walking in is judging the people they see to evaluate how your gym rolls.

Make everything as inviting as possible in those first few moments, because this is yet another time where it is critical to make a positive first impression.

We get a lot of appointments with people who have checked out other gyms but walked away because they were unwelcoming and looked scary.

STEP 2: ESTABLISH RAPPORT

They're through the door and have been welcomed, but now you need to establish a rapport with your prospect.

You often hear the top business coaches talk about how clients need to like and trust you before they will do business with you. This is very true. When was the last time you did business with someone you didn't like or trust?

Get a conversation going by asking open questions – ones that can't be answered with a simple yes or no. Many gym owners make the mistake of leading the conversation by talking about the classes and programs and barely pausing for breath, rather than taking the time to actively listen to what the visitor has to say and then tell them what they need to hear.

When you ask open-ended questions, you can discover exactly what they are looking for. Once you know that, you can use your avatar and message research to tailor your message to look like the go-to place for them.

Here are some good questions to ask.

A) What brought you in here today?

This is a hugely powerful question to ask. People don't drive across town to just check out a business; they are looking for something specific them.

You need to find out what got them to finally come in and book a consultation. Their response will help you understand what their "why" is. This information needs to guide the tone and approach you take with the rest of the consultation process to get the best chance of success.

Pay close attention to what you're told. Avoid the temptation to drift off and lose the thread of the conversation because you're hung up on what to say next. Relax and listen to the information you're being given.

Find out what specifically they are looking for.

Then follow up with the second question:

B) *Why is that important to you?*

Let them talk and focus on them. This is another opportunity to find out more about their why.

These two questions are way more powerful than leading the conversation with closed, yes or no questions. At first, it can feel a little bit awkward, but when you realize you are asking these questions to genuinely help the prospect out, you'll find you quickly relax and find your feet with it.

Keep things simple at this stage so you can remember the key information you're told. You'll be delving deeper into your prospect's motivations later, and you'll have an opportunity to jot some details down then.

STEP 3: REAFFIRM WHAT THEY TOLD YOU

Reaffirming is the easiest way to show you've been listening (everyone loves being listened too) and also to explain they are in the right place to get the help they need.

After they have told you how they feel and what they are thinking, they are looking for reassurance that you can help.

By accurately restating what they have told you and explaining how you can help, you demonstrate that you and your staff are the experts who will help them reach their goals.

STEP 4: GIVE THEM A TAILORED TOUR OF THE FACILITY

Once you know your prospect's requirements, you can highlight the aspects of your facility that offer exactly what they said they were looking for on a tailored tour.

What's more, that tour serves as another chance to find out more things they are interested in as well as detailing again how your facility will be perfect for them.

Keep it simple and don't get into long-winded talks. Give the tour based on what they are looking for and stay focused.

TIP: It goes without saying you should know the key benefits of your facility for each of your avatars before conducting a tour. Make sure to go over the highlights of your gym with your staff, and include detailed instructions in the operations manual. You can role play this to get some experience.

The tour is 100% about the prospect and not what you want to talk about. For example, if your prospect says they are nervous of getting hurt, make sure you show how the mats you use are extra thick for safety. Or if they are new to the area and want to meet new people, introduce them to a friendly student of a similar age with similar goals. You get the picture.

Some of your prospective students will be keen to compete, so a stop at the trophy cupboard and photo wall makes sense. This is an opportunity to brag on your team and show them medals and belts. People love to see success. Highlight some examples that could relate to them. Even those who aren't interested in competitions will be excited to be training with a winning team. With these folks, don't go overboard as this is a small part of the tour for them.

If the prospect is interested in weight loss, show them a picture of a student success story that is similar to them. We discussed how to set this wall up in Chapter 6. Make this tour all about losing weight and talking about students who have done what they want to do. Maybe you've got yourself back into shape too. Tell them about that.

STEP 5: FULLY UNDERSTAND THEIR NEEDS

Continue to gather information about your prospect while conducting the tour. Don't make the mistake of talking to current students too long and ignoring the person you're supposed to be welcoming. Keep the focus on them and make a note of those important details being shared with you.

From Step One, you should already know what brought them in and why that is important to them. Reinforce that and see if any other needs pop up. Make sure to listen as much as you talk on the tour.

A great way to keep it fun and memorable is to introduce them to current members, who should confirm everything you have been telling them. Always talk about when you get started training, when you're on the team, etc. Let them know they will be a part of something.

The tour is also a chance to ask some wider questions. Have they trained before? Who is their favorite fighter? What do they do for a living? Married? Kids?

You also need to find out their health on the tour. Do they have any ongoing health issues? Discuss the minor ones that you can work around. If they are major ones, ensure they have spoken to their doctor and have approval to train to protect you from liability. These could be issues such as heart problems, back problems or pregnancy. Ask your insurance company what is and what is not covered in your gym's policy.

STEP 6: DECIDE ON THE MOST PRESSING NEED

It's almost your turn to lead the conversation. Before you take control, make sure you know your prospect's most pressing need. This will make your sales presentation so much more powerful and much less confusing.

This is critical to boosting your conversion rate. When you sense it is time to present your membership options to them, you need to know exactly what to focus on.

After putting all that effort into tailoring the consultation to them, don't shoot yourself in the foot by overwhelming your prospect with a bazillion options.

STEP 7: HAVE A SIT-DOWN CONSULTATION

Your tour has done the heavy lifting and enabled you to share your message, and relate it to what your prospect is looking for in a natural and relaxed way.

You know what's important to them, what program they are interested in (or a good fit for) and what they are looking for from you. This will make your sit-down consultation go so much more smoothly and gain your more students.

Make sure you have a nice quiet area to do this where you can talk shop. Keep thinking welcoming, not scary.

This is the last chance to gather more information about the person if you need it.

At this stage, your prospect will want to view the schedule and see the prices before making a final decision.

Start by using the answers you got to your open questions earlier to demonstrate you understand their needs.

For example with the "what brought you here" question, you might say:

"Now, Tom, you said getting in shape is what brought you in today. Is that correct?"

For the "why is that important" question, you might say:

"You said that you need to get in shape because you don't want to take blood pressure medication and I can understand that."

Next, you confirm that they are in the right place and that you have a solution to their problem. They want you to reaffirm this so they can make a decision and not be left wondering.

If the person is a good fit for the program they enquired about, show them their classes on your schedule.

Sometimes they are not a good fit for the program, which is fine. Suggest an alternative that better suits their needs and explain why you have made that recommendation.

If they didn't have a specific program in mind when they booked their consultation, again, explain your reasons for recommending the one that you have.

Always sell the specific benefits of the program for that client. Don't bore them to death with tons of details.

In our MMA classes you are going to be getting a great workout and help you lose weight, so you can see if your doctor will take you off blood pressure medication. Every day you train you will be learning how to defend yourself and gain confidence in your new skills.

It's all about what's in it for them. This is why you dig deep with the questions. You have to show that you can meet that burning "why" within them. You don't just want their money, right? You want to change their life for the better. You have to know what they are looking for and confirm that your gym is the place for them to achieve that goal.

Once that's done, you need to seal the deal.

STEP 8: GET THEIR AGREEMENT

It's time to ask some closed questions because you want them to say, "Yes!"

As you show them the timetable, you want to use some specific questions to move them from being interested in joining to being committed.

A) Is this something you can see yourself doing?

This question gets them to mentally visualize themselves doing this. They may have come in nervous and not sure that they could do this. But you want them to say out loud that *yes* they can see themselves doing this.

B) Can you see how this program will get you the results you want?

They want results and they want to know that your gym can help them achieve them. You should have built up so much value with your tailored tour and shown them enough social proof that you can help people achieve results that they will answer *yes* to this question too.

C) Are you ready to get started?

Before you present prices, ask this question. If they say *yes* you reply:

Great! May I show you our membership options?

If they say, "*Well what are your prices?*", you reply:

I was just about to go over those. May I show you our membership options?

This will put them at ease that you are not here to strong-arm sell them. You should have built up so much trust in you that they want to join.

STEP 9: CLOSE THE DEAL

Many gym owners say that they don't like sales. If that's you, relax! To me, this process isn't even sales. Let me explain my take on this.

These people came to you looking for a solution to their problem and you showed them how you are a perfect fit. Now, it just comes down to if they can afford your classes. You do not have to rely on slimy sales tricks. Just follow this system.

Again, use some simple and friendly questions to subtly convert them into paying members.

Start by asking...

Can you make any of these?

Go over the schedule and circle the classes they are interested in. Then ask if they are able to train two to three times per week? (You need a yes to this question before you move on. I find progress is slow with weekly classes and it just doesn't work for the student. You can learn what to do if it's a 'no' in Step 10).

Next, confirm the key details one last time.

Great Tom, you said you can train 2-3 times per week and you are looking to lose 10lbs and I know we can get you there. Let's look at some membership options for you.

You now need to cover the pricing. This is straightforward. Simply show them your membership pricing options. This should be on nice laminated paper or an iPad. Make it look good and high quality. A crumpled bit of paper with coffee stains on it is not going to cut it.

You'll need two sets of prices – one for your annual option and another for your monthly option.

I like to present the annual one first, because it will save them the most money. People love savings.

Then, I show the monthly one for the people who can't afford so much up front. In their mind, they are already running the numbers about the two options.

Now ask only one thing:

Which option works best for you?

Then shut up and don't talk – let them decide and choose! This is where so many sales are lost. The first person to speak loses. Literally, just sit there and let them pick. If you keep talking at them, you interrupt their thinking or slip up by getting nervous and saying something you shouldn't. Talking at them means they will usually end up doing the dreaded *let me think about it...*

Once they have decided, take payment there and then for the option they prefer.

STEP 10: GETTING PAST NO

My process gets the majority of people signing up, so it's unlikely you'll get a no. But if you do, here's how to turn that around.

If they don't sign up or need to think about it, that's OK. But dig deeper so you can find out what their objection is at that point.

I understand, just so I can help you what do you need to think about?

Find out what it is and have alternative options ready. You need to know these off by heart – don't try and think something up on the fly, you'll come unstuck.

Here are some of the ones I offer:

'I can't train that often' objections

A common one is they don't know if they can attend at least two times per week. Tell the prospect:

We offer a once-a-week option for this program and you can upgrade to a regular membership if and when you're ready.

'I can't afford it' objections

Find out if it's the annual or the monthly option they are interested in. If they need to wait until their paycheck hits, simply offer them the chance to delay payment a few days. You could offer a three-month payment plan for the annual package rather than taking all the money in one hit. You could take a small deposit to secure their place on the next program to get them committed.

If they still want to go, it's time to politely close the session. It's important to make it a good experience. Don't end on a low note.

Thanks for coming to see me today. What would be a good day for us to catch up?

Don't take it to heart – some people just need longer to make up their minds and that's all there is to it.

Make sure they are on your "did not sign up" follow-up system. You can keep the relationship going with emails or your newsletter. Keep dripping content to them. Do not give up unless they unsubscribe.

TASK 9: CREATE YOUR KILLER CLOSE PROCESS

Download the template form and tweak it to suit your needs. (Resource name: initial consultation template)

- look at your facility and decide how you will run the tour
- what steps are done where
- pick out what to highlight to the prospect based on their needs – some prospects will be parents, some competitors, some into health and fitness and others into socializing
- walk through your gym and identify the best places to talk about these topics
- settle on where you need to put your social proof information
- carry out some dry runs and role plays to practice – video yourself if you're on your own so you can review your delivery.

CLOSE

You are armed with the systems to get more members and handle objections to grow your gym. Now we need to get to boosting that bottom line in your gym.

HOW TO MAKE MORE MONEY

You have learned how to turn your gym's finances around. But there are ways for you to make even more money from your facility to maximize your profits.

Bringing in new members is the lifeblood of your gym. You always need to be adding new students since others will choose to leave, that's just the nature of the business.

But this is why you need to be marketing and spending money on advertisements consistently. Never back off on this to save money as it will hurt you in the long run.

THREE WAYS TO BOOST YOUR INCOME

BOOST YOUR CONVERSION RATE

Your advertising is going to bring prospects to your gym. You've learned that the better you get at signing those prospects up, the more money you'll make. Have a look at Tables 1 and 2 in Chapter 3 for a refresher. This is the quick win to help you make more money, so make sure all of your staff members are trained to handle consultations.

GENERATE MORE REPEAT SALES

Another key number is your retention rate. Once you've got your students, you need to keep them. It's a lot cheaper to keep a current student than to bring in a new one.

One of the best ways to keep your retention rate nice and high is to keep on top of those daily and monthly SOPs. Also, remember to take an interest in your members – learn their names and smile when they arrive. These little things matter.

As well as offering excellent customer service to keep people spending money with you, you can also offer new experiences and upgrades.

OFFER MORE SERVICES

Let's be clear, this is not all about raking in cash. You have to genuinely care about your students and have great programs to help them. Everything you charge for has to be good value for money and be delivered to the same high standard.

PRIVATE LESSONS

This is a great way to help your students who need and want additional training. You can offer private lessons and so can your instructors. Just make sure to charge your instructors a percentage of the lesson to cover your gym costs and increase revenue if they are independent contractors.

If they are employees, you handle payments and pay their percentage via payroll. Nobody should be teaching private sessions from your gym and not paying to use the facility.

GUEST INSTRUCTOR LESSONS

Do you have some guest instructors you could bring in and have them teach a class? Then, you guys split the money. This is also a great way to network.

EVENTS

There are two options for events you can run at your gym: seminars and workshops. You can run these yourselves, with your staff or with guest instructors.

SEMINARS

Typically a seminar will last a few hours. You can bring in other instructors to teach your students to keep things fresh for them.

Seminars are a great way to cover a series of related topics in more depth. Just make sure your speakers are not taking all of the money and you are getting paid a percentage. Do it as a joint venture. You are bringing the venue and the people, and they are bringing the expertise.

WORKSHOPS

I really like workshops. It's an opportunity to cover something specific in more detail. As you're just covering one topic, it would be shorter than a seminar and cheaper to attend. If you teach it, you can keep all of the money. If an instructor teaches it you can split it with them.

TURN EVENTS INTO PRODUCTS

Record the workshops and seminars if you can. You can then convert the audio and video into physical CDs and DVDs. Also, you can offer them as MP3 and MP4 digital downloads.

Now you have a product that you can sell to students and a worldwide audience if you make them available online.

An excellent way to sell your digital products to prospects and students is via a membership website. Have a look at Udemy.com and Thinkific.com for some ideas.

TIP: As a bonus, you can take bits of any of these seminars and workshops to make blog and social media content that you can use to market your school. Remember, you always need to be putting out content. It's a fundamental part of your organic marketing strategy. Share your video clips directly on social media and embed them into a blog post. I also recommend to having your videos transcribed for those people who prefer to read and to make your information search engine friendly. The online service at www.rev.com is a great place for getting transcriptions and captions done quickly and cheaply.

PARTNERING WITH RELATED BUSINESSES

Teaming up with another local business is a great way to help both of you out by getting in front of each other's audience.

One simple thing you could do is put up their advertisements in your reception area, and vice versa. A good example would be a sports shop or a sports massage center where the people who visit will be interested in your products and services.

Have a think about sharing the cost of flyers or banners. If your gym is in the same building as the juice bar, perhaps you could go halves on your campaigns.

When you approach the business owner, make sure to talk about the benefits of collaborating. Mention specifics where you can – *how would you like to get your business in front of 200 fitness fanatics by putting a poster up in my gym?* Offer them more exposure and awareness – who wouldn't want that for free? It's a no brainer! You market them to your clients and they market you to theirs. It's a win-win for everybody. As Homer Simpson would say, *Woo Hoo!*

There is another benefit to this strategy. When they display your poster, it automatically gives you credibility with their audience and they will trust you. No one deliberately recommends a service that sucks. This means the partner business's customers will be more open to your offers and checking you out.

This swings both ways of course. Make sure you work with businesses that provide an excellent service and have a good reputation. If you recommend a business where someone has had poor service, it reflects badly on you.

REFERRALS AND COMMISSIONS

Another option is to offer other local businesses commissions for referral business they send your way – and vice versa.

This can be a casual set up where they refer people to you and you refer people to them. Alternatively, you can offer commissions, which is great if one business gets more referrals than the other.

In my experience, it's been highly advantageous to reach out to these types of business.

Sports massage therapists

Sports massage centers are often willing to send gift cards to be given away at special events. You can also pay them for referrals and you can return the favor by promoting their business to your members.

Cryotherapy centers

I have had a lot of luck working with cryotherapy centers. They are new and exciting so people want to check them out. See if you can get your members discounted rates and let them know you will also pay them for referrals.

Chiropractors

This is a great one as most people will need their service at some point in their lives. Have your flyers up in a few and also pay them for referrals.

PAYMENT IN KIND

Even if you don't get direct referrals, most of these businesses will give you free treatments and stuff. This is always nice

We have a deal with a local chiropractor that allows me and my instructors to get free treatments. In return, we have a banner in our foyer recommending them. It's a nice bonus and my staff love it.

TASK 10: MAKE A LIST OF BUSINESSES TO APPROACH

Contact up to 20 local businesses that share your customer base. To save time, I have created a template email/letter that you can customize. (Resource name: approach businesses letter)

SELL CLOTHING

An excellent way to boost your bottom line is by selling clothing. You can quickly make some sales with a special edition t-shirt. Make sure you have a good margin and do a pre-order. We get $500-$1,000 of straight profit each time we do this.

You want to make sure your clothing options match what your avatar is into wearing. That's why I love pre-orders. Nothing worse than ordering a bunch of clothes that no one buys. That just leaves you with an inventory, no profits and less money to spend on growing your business.

If you just want a few t-shirts printed, for your staff to wear for example, go to a print-on-demand company to make you a small batch.

A huge bonus with clothing is that it's a walking advertisement for your brand. Just make sure it's tasteful and not a billboard.

TIP: A clothing line is nice to have, but if you have a struggling gym you should spend your money on refining your Facebook advertising before putting cash into having t-shirts designed! It might flatter your ego, but it's not good business sense.

GET STUDENTS TO STAY WITH YOU LONGER

The big goal of making more money is to get your students to stay with you and train for a long time.

This seems like a no-brainer but many instructors just do not seem to care about their students. This practice will shorten the amount of time they train with you.

You want to focus on them having a great experience and always learning. This will have the bonus of you making a lot more cash.

In Chapter 6 you learned about finding new staff among the people your classes. By having more students who stay longer, you will have more to choose from and really get the best ones.

We all got into this to train and how awesome does it feel to be on your mats with a bunch of talented and experienced training partners?

That's a bonus that money can't buy.

Having a strong student base will give you peace of mind as long as you keep your expenses under control. This will help you during the slow times of the year when you don't get as many new students. You don't want the sort of feast or famine gym when a bunch of people join in January to get in shape, and they've all lapsed by the start of February!

A strong student base also makes planning and budgeting better. You need to know your numbers and plan accordingly. Build up savings so you have extra money if things get slow.

When you are confident you can retain your students, it's much less stressful spending money on bringing in new ones. This will also help you avoid the temptation to cut back on your advertising as you know you'll be able to cover the bills for another couple of months.

STRATEGIES FOR BOOSTING RETENTION

First and foremost, focus on building a sense of community. People want to feel like they belong. Do you have a private Facebook group for your members to interact and get tips? If not, get one set up. It's a quick and easy way to build up a community – and it's free.

Hit your email list at least one time a week with current events, tips and more. Ensure it's interesting and not just a boring newsletter.

Have a fun team-building event every three months. You have so many options here – paintball, bowling, cookout, laser tag, movie day, and so on. Have fun outside the gym.

Offer "refer a friend" programs where they get something for bringing in a new member. These leads cost you nothing, and they are both likely to train longer if they train together.

Contests are a lot of fun and generate a buzz around the gym. Here a couple of challenges that our students love:

- get in shape for summer
- beat the holidays

Focus on weight loss and getting in better shape. Just make sure to have a few good prizes!

Always keep refreshing your program curriculums. Do not teach the same thing over and over again or ask the students what they would like to learn today. They are paying you as the expert to teach them, and you need to be organized. A varied curriculum also makes the classes more fun because there's always something different to learn.

Having good systems in place in your SOPs will help cut down on cancellations and make your members happier. Your staff should know how to address any issue a student might have and know how to help them resolve it and feel good about it.

As soon as you know someone has a concern or hints they might leave, send your "exit email" before they cancel, not after. This one is huge. My gym only takes cancellations over email. This gives us a paper trail, so everyone knows the process and gives us one more chance to save the student.

In the email, ask them why they are quitting and if you can do anything for them. About half of them will give you a legit reason and you can work on those.

Once you know why they are quitting, try to find a solution for them to keep training. It could be as easy as changing them to a twice a week program, moving their payment date two weeks or splitting up their payments. It all depends on how creative you can get, but it makes a big difference. If you save one person paying $150 monthly, that is an extra $1,800 a year you have retained just by asking a few open questions.

IMPROVE YOUR FACILITY

When there's extra revenue coming in make sure to reinvest it in your facility.

The nicer your gym is, the higher the perceived value and the higher the prices you can command. People don't mind paying more for quality. Remember the Apple store and run down hotel examples from Chapter 6? Make sure you're not like the hotel!

In your monthly SOPs, you are looking out for broken, worn out and missing stuff. You also need to keep your eyes peeled for opportunities to create a better experience and training environment for your members.

Finally, got the money to get your signage fixed? Do it. Make sure you use this extra cash to put those things right.

CLOSE

You are now making more money with a mixture of the options you have learned in the past few chapters.

But it is important for you to know the key numbers to track in your business to make sure you measure how well those strategies are working. Let's break that down next.

HOW TO TRACK KEY NUMBERS IN YOUR BUSINESS

Numbers can be boring and few people like math (I'm one of the exceptions, lol!). Make this a game and try to get a better score each month – then watch your gym and bank account grow.

Many gym owners don't actually know the numbers they should to keep track of how their business is doing. This is why they are struggling and not growing as fast as they want to.

It's so simple, yet so often neglected.

To make sure you don't get overwhelmed by the numbers, start simple and just track a handful of simple indicators. You can then add more as you go.

The simple equations in this chapter give you powerful tools and information that will allow you to make big decisions faster and easier.

To help build your confidence and get you up and running, I have put together a spreadsheet that does all the heavy lifting for you. (Resource name: tracking spreadsheet).

Start tracking your inquiries and consultation conversions. The other things can follow on as you strengthen your business.

I've explained the numbers you need to track in priority order.

Begin with the two essential numbers you must have on hand – your customer lifetime value and average monthly transaction value. These two show how strongly the heart of your business is beating – is your gym thriving or on life support?

Once you are using the heartbeat figures, work through the others in the order they are introduced. Don't try to do too many at once. Keep it simple so you can do it consistently.

YOUR BUSINESS HEARTBEAT

The most important number is the customer lifetime value (CLTV). This is the total amount of money your average student will spend training with you. Always bear in mind this amount is usually a lot larger than your monthly membership subscription.

$membership + $workshops + $seminars + $merchandise = $CLTV

For example

7 months at $150 + 1 seminar at $40 + 2 shirts $20 and 1 Gi $50
= $1,160 customer lifetime value.

Next is the average monthly transaction value (AMTV). This is how much the average monthly payment amount is per member.

$$\$total\ monthly\ revenue/members = \$AMTV$$

For example

$$\$20,000\ revenue/150\ members = \$133\ AMTV$$

When you track this you will usually be surprised to see it's lower than your standard monthly membership rate. Family, military, police and any other discounts will lower this amount.

That's OK, but you need to know the number to work with. You don't want to budget off your monthly rate unless it's the same as your AMTV.

Using these numbers will show you how much you can spend to acquire a new student and make big financial decisions about advertising, expanding and/or remodeling.

I can spend up to $250 a month to acquire a new student, basically 100% of the first month. In an aggressive market or time, you can go a lot higher than that.

$$\$CLTV - \$member\ acquisition\ cost = \$profit$$

Most gym owners are afraid to spend money to get new members. What if I told you to give me $250 and I will give you $910 back?

$$\$1,160\ CLTV - \$250\ acquisition = \$910\ profit$$

Would you take that offer all day long? I would.

TRACKING HEARTBEAT TRENDS

Trends help you understand what is happening at any one time, and what is likely to happen with your finances. Do you see a pattern emerging of when your sign-ups are high or low? What months are your sales the highest and lowest? Knowing these two stats is crucial for planning.

You probably know seasons can affect your bank balance, but do you really track it and plan accordingly?

Here are a couple of big things I do depending on the time of year.

January to April: The gym is growing fast and sales are good so I do my remodeling, purchase new equipment and just make the gym better.

November and December: Usually a lot slower so I plan ahead. I work to get ahead on all of my bills, so I don't suffer during those slow months. This really cuts down on my stress in the slack times.

Knowing your key numbers, trends and seasonal effects makes planning so much easier and reduces stress. Don't wing it month by month and hope it all works out.

OTHER STATISTICS TO TRACK

As well as your CLTV and your AMTV, there are some more things you need to keep an eye on such as:

- student numbers
- expenses
- marketing campaigns

When looking at trends, helpful time frames to monitor are monthly, quarterly and annually.

If math brings you out in a cold sweat, relax. The spreadsheet handles all the analysis – just plug your numbers in.

STUDENT STATISTICS

Here are some key numbers you can track for your students. You do not have to do them all, just start with a couple and keep adding the ones you want to track.

Total student numbers in a given month

This is easy to track and gives you some real-time information on how you're doing.

You should always know your current number of students and if that is higher than last month and last year. Keep an eye on this so you know when you really need to ramp up your marketing.

Weekly attendance

Is this number trending up or down? Weekly attendance gives you information on the number of people training. People might be paying you, but are they turning up?

Attendance and absences rates

Make sure to keep an eye on people who are missing class and follow up with them ASAP. Checking in with them shows you care about their results. It also gives you an opportunity to identify and solve any problems within your control, rather than letting them snowball and seeing your member quit altogether. Do not let them fall through the cracks.

Reasons for leaving

When you follow your SOPs exit procedure, you will be asking those open questions about why people want to quit in your exit email. If the person goes on to leave, you will know their reason. It's important to track those reasons so you can resolve them if need be. For example, is there a frustration with a particular instructor? Can you retrain that person to do a better job or replace them? Is there a common complaint about a program? Can you change the curriculum? Could alterations to your SOPs remedy something?

TIMEFRAME STATISTICS

Let's look at money statistics with time frames.

Total sales

This is quick and easy to track with your bank statement and spreadsheets. Look at this per month, per quarter and per year and compare the difference to your current figure. The monthly and quarterly figures might change depending on your marketing efforts and seasonal trends, which is understandable. One thing you always want to aim for is to beat last year's annual total for your gross sales. That shows you're getting better at what you do.

Profit percentage

Do you know your monthly profit percentage? This is basically the amount of money that you make each month from your gym. Don't worry, I am going to show you how to start off very small and build it up from there.

This was a game changer for me. You can start off with as little as 1% every month and change your business. I actually recommend 1% just to get comfortable if you have not been pulling money out of your gym.

I learned this from the excellent book Profits First by Mike Michalowicz. It's such a simple system that allows you to do so much more with your business.

Here is a quick example: Sales – Profits = Expenses. You do the profits as a percentage. You can simply start small with 1% of sales going into a business savings account two times per month. The goal is to keep increasing that percentage and get over 20%.

Now you can build an emergency operating fund and start taking money out of your business savings every quarter to fund your retirement. Make sure you read that book to get the full system but this is a quick start for you.

TIP: I recommend you do this and the rest of the student stats monthly.

SALES AND MARKETING STATISTICS

You want to have a marketing plan that your staff follow. Make sure that it's written down and everyone knows the sales targets that must be met.

Calls to action responses for your initial consultation process are one of the most important things you can track. You want to make sure all of your marketing is paying off. This is the first number in our key statistics.

Consultation appointments booked

Next is the number of consultations. With your web analytics, you can track the percentage of people who see the schedule page and go on to make an appointment.

Consultation no shows

You should track the number of no shows for two reasons. Firstly to follow up with them and aim to reschedule, and secondly to track the percentage of appointments that showed up. You need that number to know how well you're doing converting visitors into buyers in your initial consultation sessions.

Did and didn't sign ups

This is the big number. How many sign ups did you get? This gives you the closing percentage. This is one of the most important numbers to track as it quickly tells you how well your initial consultation strategy is working and if your marketing is attracting the right sort of prospect.

When you track by the staff member running each consultation, you can identify your stronger sales performers in your team.

Make sure to follow up with the people who didn't sign up using your SOPs process. Just because they did not sign up now does not mean they won't later on.

ADVERTISING SPEND AND PERFORMANCE STATISTICS

You need to track your advertising spend and results. This is a key component of your monthly budget.

Total ad spend

What is your total ad spend for the month? Are you on budget or not? What is your ad spend on each platform (Facebook, Google, Instagram, etc...)?

Where are the leads coming from

Where are you getting most of your leads from? Track the numbers for each platform you market on.

How much are the leads costing per platform

You want to know how much the average lead is costing per platform so you can know which ones need adjusting. If a platform is not producing then it's time to lower that ad spend.

Is your ad spend significantly less than the revenue from new customers

Keep an eye on this number as it gives you good control over your budget.

Example: Ad spend $1,000 for the month.

10 new members x $199 = $1,990

$1,990 sales - $1,000 ad spend = $990 front-end profit

You get new students and didn't lose money on the front end!

EXPENSES

My gym owner clients are told to track key expenses in their monthly budget. These numbers should be pretty fixed, but you need to keep an eye on them.

Some of the main ones are rent, payroll, taxes, utilities, advertising, equipment, etc.

Track these in a spreadsheet and make any adjustments as the numbers change. You need to know what the monthly spend is at your gym. Each month the goal is to make a profit.

PRO SHOP SALES

Another figure to track is your pro shop sales. Selling t-shirts and gear can boost to your bottom line and give you more money to work with. Look at what's selling well and what's underperforming.

The key to profitable merchandising is having a high level of sales to keep turning your money over quickly to buy more stock. You don't want cash tied up in inventory that's not selling. You may have to heavily discount or write off your unpopular stock to make space for the more profitable lines.

This is why I like pre-sales of my stock – it always makes sure it's a profitable activity.

FACILITY TRACKING

Remember our facility walk-through and listing of all the things that need to be repaired or replaced? This is where you hold your staff accountable.

You or the gym manager needs to go through the gym with the list and mark off everything that was done and then address the ones that were not done. Sometimes it's just too much and needs to be moved to next month. Just make sure to always be making your facility nicer.

Make a note of how many things are being done correctly and how many are missing the mark.

CLOSE

There's a lot of numbers to take in. You don't have to track it all at once, but you do have to start. This will make it so much easier to know the pulse of your gym. Now it's time to implement what you have learned.

DO THIS STUFF

Just reading this book is not going to fix the issues you face. To grow your business, you need to implement what you have learned. Don't let the number of tasks before you overwhelm you, but you need to take action.

Start off very small with one task and then add another and another. Soon you will have a beast of a gym running smoothly.

Before the finish, let me remind you of some key factors to success.

Patience, Grasshopper

All the techniques in this book depend on having a clearly defined target market and a killer message to hook them in.

Take the time to really dial in on your market and your message. This is won't cost you anything other than time but will provide the biggest long-term value.

Some of these steps can be boring but don't rush them. Make sure to understand and implement them. Then work on your SOPs and delegation, so someone else is doing the work for you.

Write down what you need to work on

Grab a sheet of paper and just start writing all of the things you can do to improve your gym. Free stuff, expensive stuff – just write everything down. You want to free your mind up to focus on solutions, not have this stuff bouncing around in your brain day and night. This mental space will help you plan and prioritize.

Take baby steps if finances allow

Once you have your market and message dialed in and you have some cash to spend, it's time to get your paid traffic started.

Start small and scale up. You need to test and refine as you go. This greatly reduces the risk and the stress of getting it wrong at first. If you quickly burn all your cash on heaps of weak campaigns, you're going to be in trouble. As your sign-ups increase, you are able to spend more on your marketing. Don't get complacent and lower or halt your marketing activities just because you're doing OK for now. It needs to be consistent.

Fix one area at a time

Do not try to fix everything at once. Focus on one area at a time and cross it off your list before you move onto the next one. Stay focused on that area until it's done.

If you try to sort out your market, your message, filling in a bunch of numbers in a spreadsheet, revamp your website, then finish the day with a light bit of sanding and painting in a week – you're going to get burned out and give up.

Prioritize and be realistic. Here are some tips for that.

Once your market and message are done, look at all the areas in your gym and find your weakest point. Now work to improve that area and then on to the next weakest. Ask other people what they think the weakest point is. That can help you prioritize too.

You will see the biggest success when you fix your biggest weak spots. This success makes running your gym easier on a practical level which in time will compound in all the areas of your business. As you improve, make sure to update your SOPs and analyze your numbers, so you get even better still.

Every improvement you make in your gym will give you more and more momentum to keep you on pace to hit your goals.

You will notice students talking about all of the improvements. This is one of the most rewarding things.

Use your resources to your best advantage

Many gym owners I speak to are just not making much money and are stressed out about getting started on improving their facility. Two of the biggest things you can do are making sure your gym is super clean and focusing on consistent organic social media.

Focus on these areas and, as your income goes up, move into the areas that will cost money to implement and improve.

Giving your place a good clean and tidy up costs nothing, but makes a big difference.

Keep tracking your progress

This keeps you motivated and moving in the right direction. You know you're not just being busy for busy's sake – you are getting sh*t done and making improvements.

Write down your goals for the month and tick them off as you go. You are way more likely to hit them if you track them.

You can always run through the audit from time to time to make sure you're not slipping.

Don't get complacent

Whatever you do, don't get complacent with your efforts and slip back into old habits. Make sure you update and follow your SOPs. Do gym walkthroughs and review marketing results. Be a cheery face around the place. Lead by example and stay on top of the tasks.

Plan some rewards

Enjoy the process. Don't let the stress get to you. Be kind to yourself and recognize your achievements. Hit $10k a month and buy new equipment or mats. Improve the gym as you go so you can be more proud of your accomplishments.

Treat yourself to something nice. Maybe a few days away on holiday or perhaps visit that posh restaurant uptown.

Build a team of supporters

Building a successful and fun gym will take a team of supporters. Make sure to cut out the negative people who try to drag you down on this journey. This goes for staff and members, too.

Another group of people that can be huge when you're starting out or trying to grow are your friends and family. Ask them for help with projects and to support your gym. If you are hooking them up with training make sure they are supporting you via sharing posts, checking in and promoting your gym.

Bring in the skills you need to fix the weaknesses

Sometimes you can't do everything yourself. For example, if you suck at building websites, get someone to help do it rather than struggling on.

Maybe you can exchange a month's membership in return for some help? If you try to fix absolutely everything yourself, it will be a long and frustrating process.

Show gratitude for their help

When you do get folks to help make your gym a success, make sure to show gratitude. When I was starting out and had little money, I would have painting parties. Basically, I would buy pizza and beer when we got done painting. You would be amazed at what people will do for pizza and beer.

DO THE WORK!

I can't say this enough, *please do the work*! I promise that if you do the things I have taught you in this book, you will have more success in your gym then you ever dreamed of.

RESOURCES

Here's a rundown of the resources I have created for you, and a quick refresher on how they help.

You can download them all from here:

http://www.paulhalme.com/book-resources

AUDIT SHEET

You can download the audit sheet containing the questions from earlier in the book and make some notes as you work through. Resource name: audit.

AVATAR SHEET

The worked example in Chapter 2 helps you understand what you need to do before you fill out your own avatar sheet.

Remember to do one for each type of customer you plan to target. If you are really struggling, only aim to bring in one sort of customer to start with. Resource name: avatar.

FLYERS

There is an example of one of my flyers that I have used for kids and adult classes, and an editable template for you to lay something out quickly without having to hire a designer. Resource name: flyer.

SWIPE FILE

It's a lot quicker to use these samples when you're putting together your marketing message. I have provided a download and a series of links to help you. Resource name: copy swipe.

TIP: If you spot a competitor's advertisement and you like it, add it to your own swipe file.

WEBSITE WIREFRAMES

To help you create a website that is geared towards getting prospective members to contact you, book consultations or trial sessions, I have put together a template you can use to refine your message and your website structure. It is based on my website approach and all you need to do is customize it to suit your audience. Resource name: wireframes.

DETAILED SOPS

To kickstart your SOPS, I have included two examples I use in my business to speed up creating yours. Resource name: SOPS template.

INITIAL CONSULTATION FORM

This form is the one I use in my gym to help us through the process so that nothing important gets missed out.

As well as being a place to store customer responses, it also guides you step by step through my system – handy if you get anxious about sales. Resource name: initial consultation template.

SPREADSHEETS FOR NUMBER TRACKING

To save you needing to become a spreadsheet expert, I have put together a simple starter worksheet that stores and charts the core information you need to track in your business.

Remember to start with student enquiries and sign-ups first and then work on the other statistics, so you don't get overwhelmed with it all.

Once you've got the hang of that, there is a fuller spreadsheet to monitor more things in your business. Resource name: tracking sheet.

RECOMMENDED TOOLS

I have collated a list of things I have found to be super helpful in my business and put them in a downloadable PDF. Take a look and see which ones will help you. Resource name: tools.

RECOMMENDING READING

Profits First: Transform Your Business from a Cash-Eating Monster to a Money-Making Machine by Mike Michalowicz, available on Amazon.

KEEP IN TOUCH

Thank you for trusting me to help turn your gym around. I really do want you to succeed.

This book includes everything you need to boost your business, but I am here for you if you would like some more help.

Here's how you can get more help with your gym.

JOIN MY FREE FACEBOOK GROUP

I have a lively community of fellow gym owners, who meet up in my group called Momentum Monday with Paul. Search for it on Facebook or use this link:

https://www.facebook.com/groups/mmwpaul

HELP WITH DEFINING YOUR MARKET AND YOUR MESSAGE

If the idea of working out your avatar and what to say to them went straight over your head, I can help you sort that out.

I offer marketing critiques that assess what your most profitable market is in your local area, and then craft the perfect message to make your gym into the go-to facility for those people.

If you don't have any of this, I can do it as a done-for-you service.

If you would like to find out more, email me at:

paul@paulhalme.com

Alternatively, you can visit my website:

http://www.paulhalme.com/market-and-message

TURBO CALLS

If you want some specific advice or feedback on how to transform your gym, I offer concise and powerful coaching sessions for $97, reduced to $47 for readers.

You can pay for your appointment here:

http://www.paypal.me/paulhalme/47

I will send you a booking link on receipt.

REVIEW YOUR AUDIT AND HELP YOU FIX ALL OF IT

One of the quickest ways to resolve your issues is to let me review your audit and put together a plan of action to solve any weaknesses that are holding you back.

If you need rapid results and don't want to waste time with trial and error, I have a couple of options for you to consider.

ONLINE COACHING AND ACCOUNTABILITY

With this option, you send me your audit form and I review it and offer you some specific, practical advice. To help you implement my recommendations you also get monthly online coaching and accountability.

PERSONAL VISIT AND FOLLOW-UP

If you prefer, I can visit your facility and offer you face-to-face guidance with coaching and accountability to make sure you implement the changes needed.

To find out more about these options, email me at:

paul@paulhalme.com

or visit my website

www.paulhalme.com/audit-help

Wishing you all the best with your gym,

Paul Halme
Texas, 2017

Printed in Great Britain
by Amazon